Caspar Whitney

Hawaiian America

Something of its history, resources, and prospects

Caspar Whitney

Hawaiian America
Something of its history, resources, and prospects

ISBN/EAN: 9783337428389

Printed in Europe, USA, Canada, Australia, Japan

Cover: Foto ©ninafisch / pixelio.de

More available books at **www.hansebooks.com**

HAWAIIAN AMERICA

SOMETHING OF ITS HISTORY RESOURCES, AND PROSPECTS

By
CASPAR WHITNEY
AUTHOR OF
"ON SNOW-SHOES TO THE BARREN GROUNDS" ETC.

PROFUSELY ILLUSTRATED

NEW YORK AND LONDON
HARPER & BROTHERS PUBLISHERS
1899

BY THE SAME AUTHOR.

ON SNOW-SHOES TO THE BARREN GROUNDS. Twenty-eight Hundred Miles after Musk-Oxen and Wood-Bison. Profusely Illustrated. 8vo, Cloth, Ornamental, Uncut Edges and Gilt Top, $3 50.

To the general reader the narrative of Mr. Whitney's journey, the enormous difficulties overcome by him during his twenty-eight hundred miles of snow-shoeing and sledging, will no doubt appeal most strongly. The whole trip was a piece of daring adventure, and Mr. Whitney's familiar, confidential style makes the book not only instructive but highly interesting as a narrative. —*Christian Advocate*, Chicago.

The book is more than readable; it is live, real, in an extraordinary degree, and the most unimpressionable reader could scarce escape its spell.—*Providence Journal*.

A SPORTING PILGRIMAGE. Riding to Hounds, Golf, Rowing, Football, Cricket, Club and University Athletics. Studies in English Sport, Past and Present. Copiously Illustrated. 8vo, Cloth, Ornamental, $3 50.

A series of studies of English sports.... One of the clearest and most interesting accounts of the kind that we have ever seen, handsomely produced, with numerous and very attractive illustrations.—*N. Y. Sun*.

NEW YORK AND LONDON:
HARPER & BROTHERS, PUBLISHERS.

Copyright, 1899, by HARPER & BROTHERS.

All rights reserved.

TO

SANFORD B. DOLE

LORRIN A. THURSTON
AND
BENJAMIN F. DILLINGHAM

THREE OF HAWAII'S MOST LOYAL
AND
ENTERPRISING CITIZENS

THIS WORK

Is Appreciably Dedicated

FOREWORD

HAWAII has been recently the subject of so many books that perhaps I should apologize for adding one more to the number. Yet I offend—if offence it be—deliberately, and I offer no excuse for so doing. I went to the islands to study their industrial, social, and political status, and became acquainted with conditions with which I believe all Americans should be made familiar.

It has not been my purpose to produce either a history of or a tourists' guide to the Hawaiian Islands, but rather to give a fair idea of the islands and their people, their character and their industries, their resources and their prospects.

For many of the statistics in this book I am indebted to Mr. Thomas G. Thrum, the Hawaiian authority, and for the photographs of the various ancient implements I make my acknowledgments to Professor W. T. Brigham, Curator of the Bishop Museum at Honolulu.

C. W.

NEW YORK, *June*, 1899.

CONTENTS

CHAPTER	PAGE
I. A Reminder	1
II. The Local Political Situation	11
III. A Mid-Pacific Metropolis	31
IV. The Passing Native	47
V. From Oahu to Hawaii	70
VI. Kauai—"The Garden Island"	106
VII. Commercial Development	117
VIII. The Labor Question	133
IX. Industrial Prospects	159
X. Sugar-growing	184
XI. Coffee-planting	204
XII. Games and Feasts	222
XIII. Educating the Native	240
XIV. In Feudal Days	259
XV. Wane of Native Rule	280
XVI. Fall of the Monarchy	302
XVII. Birth of the Republic—and Annexation	314
Statistical	331
Distances	332
Population	334
Leprosy	340

STATISTICAL—*Continued*

	PAGE
REAL ESTATE	341
PUBLIC LANDS	342
EDUCATIONAL	343
INDUSTRIAL	347
RAILROADS	349
COMMERCIAL	350
POLITICAL	357
ADDENDA	357

ILLUSTRATIONS

	PAGE
KAMEHAMEHA THE GREAT . . . . *Frontispiece*	
IN THE OLD DAYS	3
ANCIENT GODS	8
ANCIENT BASKET-WORK	9
THE ROYAL CLOAK OF FEATHERS . . .	10
GOVERNMENT BUILDING, HONOLULU . . .	13
CARVED PLATTER FOR SERVING ROAST PORK . . .	15
PRESIDENT DOLE	17
POISON GOD	21
EXECUTIVE BUILDING, FORMERLY THE PALACE, HONOLULU .	23
CANOE, MODERNIZED GRASS HOUSE, AND HAWAIIAN WOMEN IN THEIR HOLOKUS	27
BISHOP MUSEUM, HONOLULU	33
CENTRAL FIRE-HOUSE	35
NUUANU AVENUE	37
BOWL SUPPORTED BY TWO CARVED HUMAN FIGURES . . .	39
THE PACIFIC CLUB	41
BOWL SUPPORTED BY CARVED FIGURE . . .	42
ANCIENT STONE ADZE	44
WAR IDOL, CARRIED ON POLE	48
FORT STREET, THE CHIEF BUSINESS THOROUGHFARE .	49
LAUHALO GROVE, HAWAII	53
CARVED FEMALE FIGURE FOR SEAT . .	57

ILLUSTRATIONS

	PAGE
A PRIMITIVE NATIVE HOUSE	59
IDOL	63
ON THE ROAD TO WAIKIKI	65
REMAINS OF AN ANCIENT HEIAU, OR TEMPLE OF REFUGE, NEAR KAWAIHAE, HAWAII	74
A BIT OF THE NEW GOVERNMENT ROAD TO HILO	76
SUGAR PLANTATION AND THE OAHU RAILROAD	79
HALF WHITE HULA-HULA DANCER AND (NOSE) FLUTE-PLAYER	82
WAIPIO VALLEY, HUNINI	85
COFFEE IN OHIA FOREST, HAWAII—THE FAMOUS HAWAIIAN FERN-TREE IN THE FOREGROUND	87
TRESTLE 120 FEET HIGH, TO CARRY CANE FLUME ACROSS GULCH ON PLANTATION ON HAWAII	91
NECKLACES—THE CENTRE ONE OF HAIR, WITH IVORY PENDANTS, WORN ONLY BY ROYALTY. OTHER NECKLACES OF SHELLS AND BONE, WITH BONE PENDANTS	95
SLEDGE FOR SLIDING DOWN HILL	97
WAILUKU, MAUI, ENTRANCE TO FAMOUS IAO VALLEY	98
HILO, AND ITS PRETTY BAY	100
WINDWARD COAST, HAWAII	103
NAWILIWILI, KAUAI	107
WAILUA FALLS—KAUAI	110
ONE OF THE FEW HILO RESIDENCES TO FIT ITS SURROUNDINGS	112
THE FERRY AT HANALEI RIVER	114
HANALEI VALLEY, KAUAI	115
HAWAIIAN SHARK-TOOTH IMPLEMENTS	118
HONOLULU FROM THE PALI — DIAMOND HEAD IN THE DISTANCE	121
ANCIENT HELMET, WOVEN OF REEDS AND COVERED WITH FEATHERS	124
OAHU PRISON (HONOLULU)—FISH-PONDS IN FOREGROUND	126

ILLUSTRATIONS

	PAGE
HAKALAU LANDING—HOW SHIPS ARE UNLOADED ON THE WINDWARD COAST OF HAWAII	128
ANCIENT STONE LAMPS	130
THE NECESSARY (INDUSTRIAL) EVIL	134
PORTUGUESE AND JAPANESE WOMEN AS CANE-FIELD LABORERS	136
HOMES OF SUGAR-PLANTATION LABORERS	138
SUGAR-MILL AND PLANTATION LABORERS' HOUSES	140
PLANTING CANE	143
PAPAYA TREES	147
SETTING OFF FOR THE DAY'S FISHING	150
THE TRAVELLER'S PALM	154
WOODEN IDOL	157
PINEAPPLE RANCH, BEFORE FRUITING	160
PINEAPPLE FIELD, IN FRUIT	163
LOWLAND TARO CULTIVATION	167
CARVED LADLE	170
BREAD-FRUIT TREE	171
UPLAND TARO	174
MAKING POI—POUNDING THE TARO	178
PULULA-TREE, FROM LEAVES OF WHICH THE NATIVE HUT IS MADE	180
ONE OF THE RICE-GROWING VALLEYS	182
AN OAHU SUGAR-PLANTATION PUMPING-STATION	185
HARVESTING THE SUGAR-CANE	187
HAULING CANE TO THE MILL	191
CANE PILED ALONG RAILROAD, READY FOR TRANSPORTATION TO MILL	195
THE RESULT OF AN EXPANDING COMMERCE—CANE HAULED TO MILLS BY STEAM-POWER	199
SUGAR-MILL AND LABORERS' HOUSES, KEALIA, KAUAI	202
A COFFEE CLEARING	205
TOPPED PLANTS AND PLANTATION LABORERS	209

ILLUSTRATIONS

	PAGE
A NURSERY	214
BRANCH OF COFFEE-BUSH, SHOWING BERRY	215
PLANTS SHADED BY CASTOR-BEANS	217
UNTRIMMED TREES, ABOUT THREE YEARS OLD	220
SLED	223
WHERE THE NATIVES BATHE AND RIDE THE SURF AT HONOLULU—DIAMOND HEAD IN THE BACKGROUND	225
NATIVE WRESTLERS	229
HULA-HULA GIRLS IN DANCING COSTUME	235
A *LUAU* IN THE COUNTRY	237
KAWAIAHAO CHURCH BUILT OF BLOCKS OF CORAL—THE FIRST NATIVE CHURCH IN HONOLULU	241
KAMEHAMEHA BOYS' SCHOOL	245
PUNAHOU COLLEGE	249
KAMEHAMEHA GIRLS' SCHOOL	251
LUNALILO HOME FOR AGED AND INDIGENT NATIVES	255
MUSICAL INSTRUMENTS	260
ANCIENT SHARK TOOTH, KNIVES, FISH-HOOKS, AND SLUNG-SHOT	262
WOODEN BASINS INLAID WITH HUMAN BONES AND TEETH	265
HAWAIIAN CALABASHES	270
WOODEN IDOL	272
IMPLEMENTS USED IN THE MANUFACTURE OF *KAPA*	273
A NATIVE FISHERMAN	275
AN UP-TO-DATE HAWAIIAN (NATIVE) RIDING-HABIT	281
THE NATIVE IN HIS ELEMENT	283
A ROYAL *LUAU* AT THE KING'S BOAT-HOUSE	289
THE KING'S BOAT-HOUSE, WHERE THE CARES OF STATE WERE DISSIPATED IN KALAKAU'S REIGN	295
EVENTIDE	297
THE THRONE-ROOM WHERE THE QUEEN TRIED TO FORCE HER CABINET TO SIGN HER NEW ANTI-FOREIGN CONSTITUTION	305

ILLUSTRATIONS

	PAGE
TAKING THE OATH OF ALLEGIANCE TO THE UNITED STATES — THE HAWAIIAN POLICE FORCE BEING SWORN IN AFTER THE FLAG-RAISING CEREMONIES	309
DETACHMENT OF AMERICAN MARINES ENTERING THE EXECUTIVE GROUNDS AT HONOLULU WITH THE OFFICIAL FLAG TO BE HOISTED OVER THE GOVERNMENT BUILDING	316
LANDING OF U. S. MARINES FROM THE U. S. WAR-SHIPS *PHILADELPHIA* AND *MOHICAN* FOR THE FLAG-RAISING CEREMONIES ON AUGUST 12TH	321
THE FLAG-RAISING CEREMONY, FRIDAY, AUGUST 12, 1898 — MINISTER SEWALL PRESENTS NEWLANDS RESOLUTION TO PRESIDENT DOLE	327

MAPS

	PAGE
THE HAWAIIAN ISLANDS — CROSS-ROADS OF THE PACIFIC	5
OAHU	72
MAUI, LANAI, MOLOKAI, AND KAHOOLAWE . . . *Facing*	74
HAWAII . . . "	78
KAUAI . . . "	82

HAWAIIAN-AMERICA

CHAPTER I

A REMINDER

THERE is destiny in our final assumption of authority in the Pacific Ocean, in the recognition—forced from us by the natural sequence of our own acts—of the laws of commercial gravity, which we had ignored so stubbornly and for so long.

The war with Spain invested the Pacific Ocean with new and potential significance for the United States; it hastened the inevitable annexation of the Hawaiian Islands; emphasized the value of an isthmian canal; illustrated the urgency of a Pacific cable; widened the national outlook, and, let us hope, broadened the view of some of our people—editors, politicians, citizens.

The need of supporting Admiral Dewey in the Philippines, after his brilliant victory in May, settled at once and for all time the long-pending Hawaiian question.

We could not send troops and ships to Manila without using Honolulu as a half-way refreshment port; so necessity accomplished what common interest failed to attain, and the Stars and Stripes were flung to the breeze at Honolulu, August 12, 1898.

It was a conclusion long sought, and suggestive of mutual benefit.

For fifty-six years union had been making. Since 1843 the United States had been notifying the world that it would not, without opposition, permit the Hawaiian Islands to yield allegiance to another nation. Daniel Webster declared that "no other power ought either to take possession of the islands as a conquest or for the purpose of colonization." Secretary of State Clayton, in 1850, warned France that "we could never with indifference allow them [the Hawaiian Islands] to pass under dominion or exclusive control of any other power."

In 1854, '68, and '73 annexation to the United States was unsuccessfully sought by the reigning sovereigns of the islands. In 1855 a reciprocity treaty with the United States was drawn up by the Hawaiians, but not ratified at Washington. Again, in 1864, '67, and '74 effort was made to conclude the treaty between the two countries, and in '75 it was finally ratified by the United States. Three times —in 1874, '89, and '93—have American men-of-war been called on to protect property and the lives of citizens at Honolulu from revolutionary mobs.

Every administration of the United States, save

A REMINDER

one only (Cleveland), from President Monroe to President McKinley, recognized Hawaii as a commercial outpost of this country, and sympathized with the annexation sentiment.

IN THE OLD DAYS

President Harrison, February 17, 1893, transmitted to Congress, with his approval, a treaty of annexation coming from Hawaii. President Cleveland, March 9, 1893, withdrew the treaty, and subsequently instituted his "policy of infamy," which, from the appointment of "Paramount" Blount, to the deliberate duplicity of Minister Willis and Liliuokalani's visit to Washington, breathed insult to John L. Stevens and misjudgment of the Hawaiian Provisional Government. Acceptance of *ex parte* testimony and of Blount's report drew bitterest criticism upon Mr. Cleveland and upon his Secretary of State, Gresham, both at home and abroad.

President McKinley, June 16, 1897, signed another annexation treaty, which was submitted to the Senate and ratified July 6, 1898—after Dewey's victory at Manila had made ratification imperative.

These are facts for Americans to remember.

The principle of annexation is no new one to the United States. It was first exploited in 1778 with invasion of the Northwest Territory, whereupon Continental Congress immediately made a virtue of necessity by founding a territorial system. Since then consent of previously existing independent governments has been obtained twice—in the case of Texas and of Hawaii. Nor is the white race in the midst of an inferior or foreign one the novel situation to us it is popularly written down to be. When we took over Louisiana in 1803 it had 42,000 inhabitants, the majority of whom understood no language but French. Florida, absorbed a few years later, and New Mexico understood little but Spanish.

As to our ability to colonize—Professor Albert

THE HAWAIIAN ISLANDS—CROSS-ROADS OF THE PACIFIC

A REMINDER

Bushnell Hart estimates that, from 1820 to 1898, 18,000,000 foreigners have come to America, and have been absorbed so completely as to make Americans of their grandchildren. The winning of the West and of the Northwest has been but a succession of colonial plantings—from the admission of Ohio in 1802.

Predominance of Anglo-Saxon in Hawaii is as sure to come as it has in Louisiana, Florida, Texas, New Mexico, Arizona, California—only it will come more slowly.

Hawaii, with China and Japan, are the only three countries in the Pacific Ocean possible to permanent white settlement—the only ones where residence brings no deterioration to the Anglo-Saxon; where his family, his home, himself, may be transplanted and thrive. Hawaii is the only country (in part) below the Tropic of Cancer where fusion of blood and influence is likely to eventuate.

And in no other way may genuine civilization be attained.

No such fusion is possible in India, Java, Sumatra, Siam, Malay Peninsula, or in the Philippines, where the white race takes up its abode for a time to rule or to make money, and where too often the mere dominance of a single type simply stimulates native vices.

Hawaii, alone of our possessions, is likely to become an American community. Here is no problem such as awaits us in the Philippines, or in Puerto

Rico, or even in Cuba, pending the establishment of stable native government, nor such a one as we faced at home with the Indian, whom we could not civilize where he stood, or protect from the ad-

ANCIENT GODS

vance of the white settler, or save from the greed of the politician.

Herein Hawaii is no new or uncivilized country. Here is no field for the missionary or the politician. The first printing-press on the Pacific coast was sent thither from Honolulu, and while Indians and buffalo roamed the "new West" at will, Hawaii furnished the California gold-hunters of 1849 with potatoes and wheat.

No wrenching of local law or upheaval of native custom attended the annexation of Hawaii. Here was a country with an established government uncorrupted; a people — the richest *per capita* in the world, and with a percentage of illiteracy lower than that of any European nation, save

A REMINDER

perhaps Prussia, and lower than that in many of our own States; a land capable of producing the majority of the products of the temperate and tropical zones; a country largely Americanized and wholly Christianized.

Hawaii's future need give us not the smallest anxiety—her politics are purer than our own, her legislators more loyal to her interests.

Strategically considered from a militant or commercial view-point, the Hawaiian Islands are unique and invaluable. They are the practical centre of an area so vast as to make impossible either mili-

ANCIENT BASKET-WORK
(Now a lost art)

tary or commercial operations across it that do not include the islands as supply and coal depot. They are a midway station in the commercial union of East and West; an ocean cross-roads where routes between Japan, China, Australia, and the American continent converge; a distributing centre of the greatest ocean of the world; the stepping-stones by which American enterprise will invade Asiatic markets.

Hawaii is the best sentinel the United States

THE ROYAL CLOAK OF FEATHERS

have or could post in the Pacific Ocean. Literally there are no men-of-war that can operate across the Pacific; few have sufficient coal capacity to even cross, and none carry enough coal to cross and operate immediately after without resupplying.

There is no more certain defence of the Pacific coast than Hawaii under the Stars and Stripes.

CHAPTER II

THE LOCAL POLITICAL SITUATION

HAWAII has suffered from the pens of the subsidized correspondent and the half-informed editor of prejudice as none other among enlightened peoples. We have read of the "hierarchic rule of the missionary element"; of the "base deception" of the few in power practised upon the many in tribulation; of the "restlessness" of the native under the changed political conditions; of our perfidy in annexing Hawaii without "consent of the governed"; of "native unanimity" for the restoration of Liliuokalani.

Honolulu is an excellent field for the reporter who seeks sensation rather than fact. Having only weekly steamer communication with the world, people in that little mid-ocean city concern themselves, rather more perhaps than those in any other English-speaking community on earth, with one another's affairs. We all know the tender solicitude of the friend who discusses our affairs—that considerate friend whom the latch-string never escapes, and with the apologetic introductory, " It's none

HAWAIIAN-AMERICA

of my business, I know, and I never discuss other people, *but* they do say," etc., etc.

When a Pacific cable puts Hawaii in daily touch with the world, its people will have more to think about and become less gossipy.

I devoted many days while at Honolulu, and painstaking inquiry at many sources, to put myself in touch with the various local sentiments on the political situation. Never did I gain so little material for so much endeavor. Not that any one refused to talk. On the contrary, all were willing and (apparently) anxious to be delivered of the thoughts, obviously burdensome. Never did men talk more and say less. I could extract positively nothing tangible upon which to base an argument or follow a line of investigation.

I should say, first of all, that among white men there is really no serious division of opinion political in all Hawaii. On all important matters touching the welfare of the islands, the judgment of those, white and native, whose opinions command attention is uniform. But human nature in Hawaii is the same as elsewhere, and therefore at Honolulu one learns of slight disagreement that satisfies itself with mild discussion at the Pacific club. In time, no doubt, Hawaii will have its Republican and Democratic parties, but at present the only party division at all discoverable is one based on *pro* and *anti* missionary leanings. And this is so indefinite it can hardly be dignified with

GOVERNMENT BUILDING, HONOLULU
Statue of Kamehameha the Great

THE LOCAL POLITICAL SITUATION

name, and so misleading as to require explanation to the non-Hawaiian reader.

The *anti*-missionary element may be described as those whites who more recently immigrated to Hawaii, and are envious of the political and commercial pre-eminence of the early settlers' descendants. The majority of this *anti* element comprises men of the smaller business interests — shopkeepers, clerks — few of whom have strong prejudices on the subject.

CARVED PLATTER FOR SERVING ROAST PORK

The minority *antis*, the agitators, who do the talking at home and supply the newspapers abroad, are political aspirants from the mainland, and a few foreigners and half-castes of vicious tendencies and absolute irresponsibility.

The *anti* element has a grievance, of course, but it concerns personal emolument more than the prosperity of Hawaii. They seek place on the governmental salary-list rather than part in the judicious guidance of the government. They offer no tenable criticism of the government; they do not pretend to deny that the ministry of the Republic administered the public affairs of Hawaii wisely, economically, ably. I could not extract a single criticism from the more intelligent members of the *anti* element with whom I talked, nor have I read one anywhere, against the ministers of the Republic and those continued in office under annexation, that could be sustained or seriously viewed.

Pressed for at least one definite objection to the appointment of Hawaii's "Grand Old Man," Sanford B. Dole, as Governor, one of the more intelligent of the *antis* said:

"The President (Dole) does not entertain enough"; and followed it by adding, "and when he was made President of the Republic he did not treat his friends well."

"How so?" I queried.

"Well," replied my informant, "he kept a lot of government department clerks in office who had for years served under the monarchy."

"Ah!" said I, "then you object to President Dole because he is not an advocate of the spoils system; you would have him turn out all the clerks, who were in no way responsible for the actions of the monarchy, and who have been in government service, some of them, for years, to make room for his particular political supporters." To which my *anti*-missionary friend demurred, as perhaps too harshly expressing his thought.

And this "missionary element," of which we hear so much—what is it? who constitute it?

One of the very wisest acts of Kamehameha II. was to give lands to the missionaries who had ar-

PRESIDENT DOLE.

THE LOCAL POLITICAL SITUATION

rived at Honolulu from New England in the first years of his reign. This resulted in the children of these missionaries, instead of being sent back to America, remaining on the islands to be educated, and growing up into the island business filled with Hawaiian interest. They learned to look upon Hawaii as home, and, as such, closely identified with their future. That is where the great difference lies in interest and in accomplishment between results here and elsewhere in foreign lands where American missionaries have gone.

Thus the commercial development of Hawaii was begun by the sons of the first missionaries, and has been to a very large extent carried on by their descendants. Other white settlers have married into these families, so that to-day those who are connected with these pioneers of Hawaiian civilization, either through direct descent or by marriage, collectively are called the missionary element, and represent at least three-fourths of Hawaii's industrial and commercial strength. With these have arrayed themselves the best of the immigrant whites.

This element, in its full strength, has been literally the salvation of Hawaii. It has been the upbuilding and the cleansing of the islands during times of extreme individual peril and uncertain governmental existence. It is the element which furnished the ministry whose first official act was to vote down their respective salaries a couple of thousand dollars each. And there is not an intelligent, honest *anti*-missionary man on the islands who does not know this, and in his heart realize how weak is the platform on which his especial clan stands.

In the last years of monarchial rule, however, and during the Republic, there were genuinely serious points of issue, and all Hawaii was really separated into two great divisions. Not missionary and *anti*-missionary, but royalists — including all the supporters of the monarchy, and *anti*-royalists, comprising the best of all resident elements, native and *anti*-missionary as well, who sought to purify the political atmosphere.

The royalists included the bulk of the natives; certain foreigners (not Americans) who either through marriage or by business engagements enjoyed peculiar and profitable advantages under the monarchy, and a few blatherskite half-castes of no standing and less regard for the country. The foreigners were actuated by promise of personal aggrandizement; the half-castes incited by vicious tendencies and the assurance of temporary livelihood, and the natives moved by a dumb tenacity to traditional ruling by natives. It is exceedingly doubtful if the natives would ever have given voice to their sentiments on the subject had they not been inflamed by agitator half-castes and supported by the foreigners.

The native has really no deep feeling on the

THE LOCAL POLITICAL SITUATION

subject; his emotional nature is easily played upon and is superficial as responsive; let but the splendid native band at Honolulu play "Hawaii Ponoi"—the native national air—and you might fancy by his pensive manner and alert attitude that he would yield his life for his country. Yet in the revolution of 1895, when Lilioukalani by force of arms sought the destruction of the Republic and her restoration to the throne, not over one hundred and forty-five natives took up arms to regain that which they have been credited with holding as dear as life itself. The natives' view of the changed political condition is purely lackadaisical.

POISON GOD

Restoration of the monarchy appealed to certain more or less worthless classes of the natives, to whom it suggested free *luaus* (feasts) and unchecked indolence, and, in candor it must be admitted, to also a few of the better native class who had been officially connected with the government.

But nothing quite so patently reveals ignorance of native character as the assertion, popular with the half-informed, that the native "harbors resentment" over what the opponents of annexation have been pleased to term his "downfall."

It seems a waste of time and space to answer criticisms that are so manifestly based on ignorance and prejudice, yet perhaps good may come of enlightenment. To begin with, then—the native had more individual right, more land privileges, and a higher wage under the Republic than under the monarchy; and annexation extends his enfranchisement through modification of the educational and property qualifications required of voters. So much for his "downfall."

The idea that the native cherishes "resentment" for deliverance from the corrupt and selfish monarchy is equally fanciful. Not that he should fully appreciate the benefits accruing from changed conditions, but that he should entertain any feeling so disturbing as resentment. The average native makes no unnecessary effort, mental or physical.

Like all seaport towns, Honolulu (though to an infinitely less degree) has had its share of dissolute wanderers, and these, sometimes foreigners, sometimes half-castes, have on occasions succeeded in getting together a handful of natives for an expression of opposition to the course events were taking. But, generally speaking, the native gives the matter of republic, or annexation, or monarchy little serious or intelligent thought. During my tour of the islands I never lost an opportunity of sounding native feeling, and almost invariably found it indifferent, with an acknowledgment, if I pushed the question, of more civil rights under republic and annexation than under monarchy, but yet a

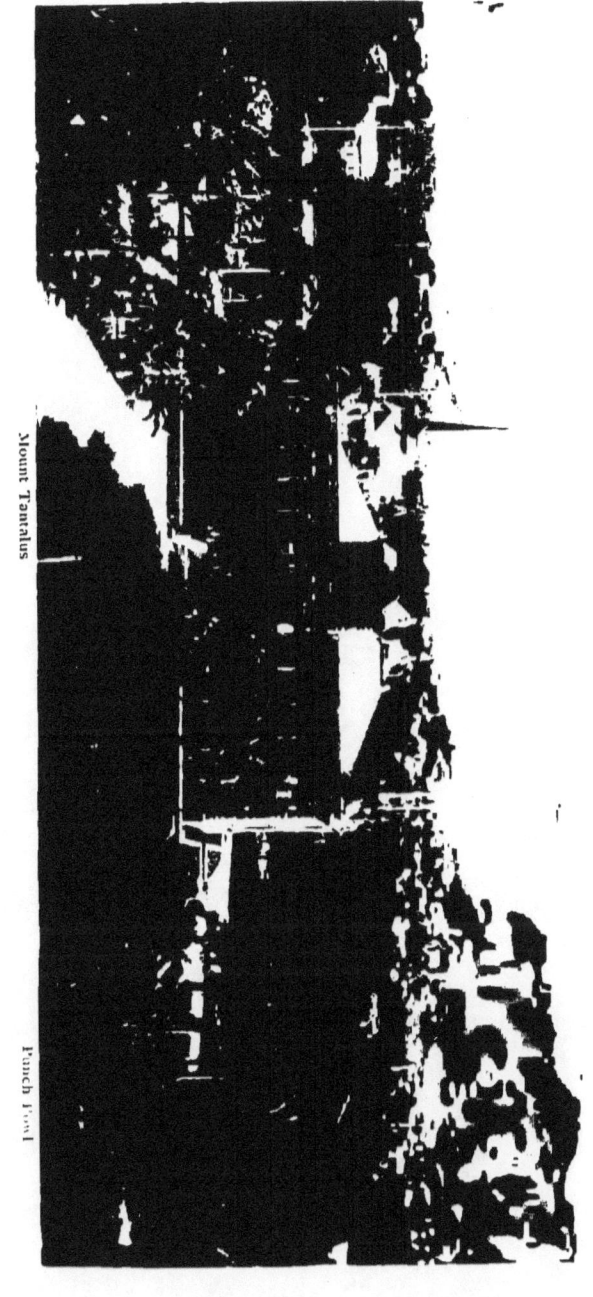

EXECUTIVE BUILDING, FORMERLY THE PALACE, HONOLULU
Characteristic Hawaiian cloud effects on the mountains in the background

THE LOCAL POLITICAL SITUATION

lingering traditional sentiment favoring native rule.

Perhaps two-thirds of the natives, if urged to a statement of preference, would give a half-hearted answer in favor of monarchy, and yet not one per cent. of them would make an unusual effort to attain that end. Not solely because of indolence, but because of indifference.

Moreover, there is no unity of native opinion on a native sovereign—there are "Queen" Emma, Kalakaua, and Liliuokalani factions, the following of the last being perhaps the smallest.

At this writing the adjournment of Congress without legislation on the subject leaves the government of Hawaii as fixed by the Newlands resolution annexing the islands. This resolution appointed a commission which, after a visit to Hawaii, submitted a report providing that the President of the United States appoint a governor of the Territory of Hawaii, a secretary, a United States district judge, district attorney, and marshal; that the legislature consist of two houses—a Senate of fifteen members, and a House of Representatives of thirty members; that the House be elected by all male citizens twenty-one years of age; that the citizens be defined as "all white persons, including Portuguese and persons of African descent, and all persons descended from the Hawaiian race who were citizens of the republic of Hawaii immediately prior to the transfer of the sovereignty thereof to the United States." It further provided that a citizen, to be eligible to vote for a senator, must own property worth $1000, or have an annual income of $600; that the chief-justice and two associate justices of the supreme court, and the judges of the circuit court, be appointed by the Governor; and that a Territorial delegate be elected.

This bill was not passed by either the Senate or the House of Representatives.

Subsequent legislation looking to the extension to Hawaii of the laws of this country passed the House, but was not voted upon by the Senate.

And now Congress, which has furnished so many remarkable spectacles, has supplied one notable among the many, in that the suggestions of the commission — Senators Morgan and Cullum and Representative Hitt — that was sent to Hawaii for the particular purpose of studying the situation and reporting on its legislative and other needs, are ignored and its report torn to pieces by men who have no personal knowledge of the subject, and seek to apply domestic remedies to foreign ills.

Thus is Hawaii under makeshift government until Congress acts definitely next autumn.

There are two things absolutely needful to Hawaii's continued prosperity and the riper development of her industries — (1) property and educational qualifications exacted of all voters, and (2) previous residence of at least three years made nec-

CANOE, MODERNIZED GRASS HOUSE, AND HAWAIIAN WOMEN IN THEIR HOLOKUS

THE LOCAL POLITICAL SITUATION

essary to eligibility for any Territorial office. Hawaii wants no carpet-bagger politicians.

The first of these is the one Congress shies at most.

One of the remarkable exhibitions attending debates on Hawaiian annexation, its government, etc., has been the unreasoning persistency with which some of our dull-witted legislators have sought to encompass broad conditions with petty provisions. Because Territories on the mainland have thrived under certain laws, they argue that a Territory four thousand miles to the east, in another clime and under another sun, must also thrive under the same laws. Because the American soldier had kept in good condition on pork at home in a temperate climate, pork was given him on his very first campaign in the semi-tropics! And with what results?

No doubt when the time comes to set up a government in the Philippines, there will not be wanting honorable gentlemen in Congress to urge the promulgation of laws that have been found beneficent in Arkansas, in Arizona, or in Idaho.

The American people would save money in the end by the establishment now of a fund for the proper education of its national legislators. Let it be called a fund for the advancement of political jurisprudence, and make its first official extravagance a round-trip ticket at least to Yuba Dam for each and every Senator and Representative whose observation of mankind has been confined to his own county fair and Washington hotel bar-rooms.

HAWAIIAN-AMERICA

It is violating no principle of the Federal Constitution to prescribe an educational or property qualification as necessary to the attainment of suffrage; on the other hand, it would be an outrage on the civilized race were the control of government, of commerce, of the interests of civilized people, to be given into the hands of the ignorant and uncivilized and incompetent of Hawaii, Puerto Rico, or the Philippines, by the failure to equalize matters through the necessary and practical provisions suggested by common-sense.

What would become of Puerto Rico if the ignorant masses of low intelligence were given each a vote? What of the Philippines, with its one million savages each enfranchised? Has our experience at home with the negro race given us no lessons on this question?

It would be cause for deep rejoicing if an educational qualification were demanded of all voters in our own United States of America.

Hawaii is not to be compared with Puerto Rico, Cuba, or the Philippines; it is civilized, educated, prosperous (as the result of the white man's work); nevertheless, its future would be seriously menaced were no restrictive provisions attached to native enfranchisement.

By all means give the native a voice in the government, but let us make sure that it be the best element and not the worst which we enfranchise.

CHAPTER III

A MID-PACIFIC METROPOLIS

FIRST impressions are usually so much nearer the heart, so much more enduring, it is comforting when they are pleasant and need not be revised. Therefore Hawaii must appeal strongly and tenderly to every visitor who has an eye for the unaffectedly beautiful, and a scrap of sentiment in his being. Nowhere may the simple story of the people and of the land be read so easily and with such confidence in its fidelity. It is amusing to compare with the tales of discontent and poverty that find their way into newspaper print the actual openness and happiness of native life in Hawaii.

The charm of the Hawaiian Islands lies in their physical characteristics—the suggestion of strength and gentleness given by their broken peaks and slumbering volcanoes, and the velvety verdure that tempts you to the hills, and begets an impulse to plunge your nose deep down in the grass for one long inhalation of wholesome earth. If your breast conceals any nature-loving relic of savagery—that savagery which hungers for actual contact, and is not content with mere picture-gazing—be assured Hawaii will reveal your passion and satisfy your desire.

All the reading-world knows by this time that the Hawaiian Islands are of volcanic origin, each with its valleys and mountains, its lowlands and uplands, its dry side and rainy side, its perennial spring and its heaven-born climate—but only those who have lingered under their influence can appreciate the subtle charm of the lights and shades on the mountains.

Hawaiian time seems divided into alternate and swiftly changing cycles of shadows and sunshine and rainbows.

'Tis well we approach this land from the sea, for so do we have opportunity to consider its attractions; and well, too, that our port of entry is Honolulu, for it is on the island of Oahu—the loveliest of all the group. Oahu has not the beautiful valleys of either Maui or Kauai, or the volcanoes and jagged windward coast of Hawaii, but it has been picturesquely fashioned with a hand both artistic and unique. Oahu leaves the impress of its individuality upon you. Once having seen Diamond Head, you never escape remembrance of its bold, naked outline; or if, driving from Waikiki, you have looked up Manoa Valley, with the sun just sinking over the island's backbone, and the drifting clouds swiftly varying

BISHOP MUSEUM, HONOLULU

A MID-PACIFIC METROPOLIS

the shades on the hills, the picture will ever after dwell in your memory.

You feel the influence of Oahu as the steamer draws near enough for your glasses to discover the

CENTRAL FIRE HOUSE

wild, weird splendor of the windward coast that culminates in the *Pali*—a different, more fascinating, scenic beauty from any you ever beheld. A sense of physical witchery, as under the insinuating influence of a rare vintage, steals through your veins as the steamer passes Koko Point, and, rounding Diamond Head, reveals the capital of the

Hawaiian Archipelago — Honolulu — with a solid rock guard at either point of its crescent-shaped harbor, the mountains at its back, and an untroubled sea at its feet.

The harbor is small and crowded. Some day, not far distant, Honolulu's principal docks and shipping with its three locks will be seven miles away, at Pearl Harbor, where there is an interior frontage of twenty-five miles, and water averaging from thirty to fifty feet in depth.

Drink your fill of the scenic beauty while yet you are off shore, for there is less of the picturesque to engage you on the landing.

Through a channel, narrow, though deep enough to admit the deepest ships of the world, you pass into the harbor, inside the coral reef that imprisons the entire water-front, and look full into the languorous landscape of many colors that plays so strongly on your fancy. And it will glow anew under your closest scrutiny—like some eyes that grow deeper and more eloquent the longer we search them.

Thus, enchanted, expectant, you stand at the ship rail while the sensuous beauties of Oahu materialize before your sympathetic gaze—until the bumping of the steamer against the low pier breaks the spell, and the dock buildings hide the scenic vision, only to disclose another, filled with native men and women — all smiling and chatting and hand-waving—with *leis* (wreaths) of various-colored

flowers around their hats and necks, and *Aloha* on their lips.

Aloha — which conveys greeting and good-will and welcome.

Honolulu is a town of engaging, not to say amusing, contrasts. It has rubber-tired hacks—and no sewerage; electric light—and no sidewalks in the residential quarter; tropical surroundings—and, for the most part, coldest of prim New England architecture; a soil capable of producing vegetables in abundance—and canned corn and tomatoes and pease and beans on the shelves in the shops; a spacious, well-built public market—and for half its space empty of stall tenants; every good reason why living should be inexpensive—and in very fact an atmosphere charged with comparative extravagance.

Not many surprises await the travelled visitor at Hawaii, but three there are in very truth, and one is deeply gratifying and two are startling;—to

BOWL, SUPPORTED BY TWO CARVED HUMAN FIGURES

HAWAIIAN-AMERICA

wit—(1) the paternal care of the native by the white-born Hawaiians; (2) the Americanization of Honolulu; (3) the industrial opportunities offered by the natural resources of the islands—and neglected.

You have been wise, from the steamer-deck, to yield yourself to the tropical seductiveness all Hawaiian views impart at distance, for disappointment awaits you on first landing, unless you have never before set foot on semi-tropical shores. Down-town Honolulu is clean, industrious, conventional, with sidewalks entirely Western, and streets that, though somewhat narrower than common in American towns of equal size, are yet much wider than those of other semi-tropical cities. There is nothing that suggests the tropics—not even the Chinese and Portuguese quarters—not even the native women in their *holokus* (as a Mother Hubbard wrapper they wear is called), or the native men in their blue cotton trousers, straw hats, and bare feet. Every shop-window suggests America; on all sides there is English speech—even the solitary beggar who accosted me in the two months of my sojourn was an American. Any town chosen at random in southern New Mexico or Arizona would disclose scenes equally tropical and more foreign, though less cosmopolitan.

But there is relief for eye and ear in the residential streets, which are those that extend straight from the heart of the town, or lie closer to the hills in the background, or skirt the shore up to the very shadow of Diamond Head. Most attractive of those running inland is Nuuanu, leading into the valley of the same name, and culminating at the *Pali*, most famous of Honolulu drives. Most delightful of those skirting the shore line is Waikiki,

THE PACIFIC CLUB

with its tempting beach, bathing, and surf-riding, and the rakish picturesqueness of its cocoanut-palms. And wherever space and care are given them bloom the flaming Hibiscus, the pendent yellow clusters of the Golden-shower, the Begonia, the ma-

HAWAIIAN-AMERICA

genta-colored Bougainvillea, overtopped and sheltered by the spreading *Ohia* and guarded by the regally Royal palm. Curiously, the rose and the violet are the only flowers that do not thrive here.

Nature has showered gifts upon these islands, and the white settlers have spoiled the urban landscape by thrusting into it their ill-suited abodes. The severe New England type of house, with its gables, its blinds, its square ends and sides, and its trim fences, is so utterly incongruous to Hawaiian environment as to be irritating. Here and there is a bungalow, fitting into its surroundings with satisfying harmony, and within five years houses have been losing much of their former severity, but the type still rules to jar the artistic sense of the visitor. Everywhere on the islands the houses suggest the dominant New England influence that even luxuriant surroundings of the semi-tropics have not softened. Honolulu has the situation and the endowments for making the most beautiful city in all the world, but it needs the developing hand of a sponser more alive to the artistic possibilities of its environment.

BOWL, SUPPORTED BY CARVED FIGURE

Yet, after all, perhaps it is hardly fair to seek an

æsthetic side of Honolulu, when are considered the dulness of artistic sense in the native, and the lack of it in the section whence came the earliest white settlers.

If from an artistic view-point opportunities have been neglected in this Polynesian capital, at least much has been accomplished in industrial development.

In 1820, when the missionaries and traders and whalers came, Honolulu was a scattered village of grass huts and about 3000 inhabitants; in 1866 its population numbered from 12,000 to 15,000, and its buildings were of adobe; or of the old grass type, now rarely seen, and only in the interior; or of coral, many of which still stand, notably a large native church. Few towns of Honolulu's population (30,000), even in the United States, are better equipped for industrial and educational life. There are business and public buildings, modern and handsome; paved streets, a public library (12,000 volumes), fire department, police, water-works, with telephone system the most obliging service I ever encountered, theatre, hospitals, asylums, public market; a notably complete museum, under the able curatorship of Professor W. T. Brigham (Harvard); homes for sailors, homes for the indigent natives; two colleges, thirty-five private and twenty-five public schools, including industrial, reform, normal, and night schools. Of churches there are about half a dozen, representing as many different denominations. There are four daily newspapers printed in English, one in Hawaiian, and, all told, daily, weekly, and monthly, there are eleven publications in English, four in Hawaiian, two each in Portuguese, Japanese, and Chinese. And it should be remembered that of the town's population over 11,000 are natives and part natives, 8700 are Chinese and Japanese, 2000 are Portuguese, leaving about 8000 whites, of whom two-thirds are Americans.

Honolulu has, in fact, everything needful to her size and importance except a really first-class hotel and a street railway that gives satisfactory service. The present street-cars are intermittent, filthy, and patronized almost exclusively by the natives. There is talk of a trolley system, which is much needed, and that would be exceedingly profitable. Meantime there is a hack system—extensive (260) and impoverishing—with a tariff calculated to bring a blush to the cheek of the most reprobate New York "cabby." Mindful, however, of what has already been accomplished, we

ANCIENT STONE ADZE

may have confidence in Honolulu's discernment for the future and of her proper adjustment to requirements.

Nor is it Honolulu alone of all Hawaii that is thus Americanized: throughout the islands one finds the same influences at work and results similar. The dominant language of the group is English—not with the British, but the American pronunciation: the newspapers come from American presses, are conducted by American journalists, and filled with American topics; the literature on the counters of the book-shops and reading-rooms is three-quarters from American publishers. The ruling social, commercial, political, religious life of the people of Hawaii is overwhelmingly American. The schools are patterned after the American system, the text-books American, and, except in the rural districts, where half-whites and natives are employed, the teachers are largely American. The President—or Governor, as he soon will be—and two members of his recent cabinet are Hawaiian-born Americans; two other members are American-born. The constitution and the laws of the late Republic were patterned after those of the United States; two-thirds of the supreme and circuit court judges and the majority of the lawyers in the upper courts are Americans. The same is true of the governmental bureaus, and of the Advisory Council.

Americans own two-thirds of the taxable property in the islands, and control equally as much of the sugar-plantation interests. Three-fourths of the foreign shipping calling at Honolulu is American — a statement that cannot be made of any other port in the world—while the inter-island steamship lines and the banking interests are entirely American.

American influence began in Hawaii with the outreaching enterprise of the expert whalers of Nantucket and New Bedford, and was spread by the little band of missionaries who for over twenty years constituted the chief body of civilized residents, and remained to shape, even at so early a day, the benevolent and ably organized institutions that were subsequently born to the country.

Americans brought commerce, civilization, education, prosperity, to Hawaii. Was there not, indeed, warrant for giving this island colony the fuller benefits of annexation?

CHAPTER IV

THE PASSING NATIVE

AND what of the native — what part is he to play in Hawaii's future? what rôle has he filled in the immediately progressive past? There has been so much maudlin sentiment expended on him, and such bias exhibited in discussion on this subject, it will be instructive, perhaps interesting, to have a glance at facts.

Hysterical writers declare the native has lost all his belongings except his dark eyes and his passion for flowers; that his patrimony has been squandered, and finally his country taken from him.

Some travellers see only the picturesque side of life and things, some only the superficial, some only the vicious—let us try, by the light of my research and travel over the islands, to view, without prejudice and without silly sentimentality, the situation as it now exists.

There is nothing so obtrusive in the written history of Hawaiian life as the contrast between the harsh treatment of the natives by their own rulers and their kind treatment by the whites. The white man's conquest of Hawaii has been through the confidence born of kindness and the peace born of education. The native never had a birthright until the influence of the white man gave it to him, for the days before the missionaries came were feudal days—when the common people were serfs, and no man owned a foot of soil except by the king's favor, and then only during the lifetime of his immediate master.

WAR IDOL, CARRIED ON POLE

Not until 1839 did Kamehameha III. proclaim his famous Bill of Rights—the Hawaiian Magna Charta—which for the first time gave uncertain land tenure to the native. Meanwhile the missionaries, who had arrived in 1820—one year after the Hawaiians had cast off idolatry—labored with indifferent success, until 1837, when a religious stir began, which, speeded by the emotional nature of the natives, resulted in pious frenzy that literally swept the islands — converting large numbers to the white man's doctrine.

The rapid and complete Christianization of the Hawaiians is one of the missionary wonders of the present century; it has no parallel in the world's history.

FORT STREET, THE CHIEF BUSINESS THOROUGHFARE

But, though he changed his religion, the native's habits remained very much the same, and though his mind was attuned to the teachings of the missionaries—the heritage of indolence and of licentiousness bore heavily upon him. He loved the sunshine, his womankind, and the opalescent water that surrounded him. Why should he work when the sea held fish, and the cocoa-palm provided drink, nourishment, and clothing? What need for toil with the papaya and the bread-trees dropping their fruit like manna every day for all the days of the year?

The indolent Hawaiian is no Polynesian novelty, but he does occupy the unique position of being the only race on the Tropic of Cancer that is losing its identity. As with the Siamese, intermarriage with stronger races is changing the Hawaiian's physical and mental characteristics; and, as with the baboos of India, education is having the somewhat similar effect of divorcing the Hawaiian (not invariably) from his early industrial pursuits. Not that the Hawaiian has an inherent tendency towards industry, but education and prosperity, and more likely the latter, I fancy, are certainly lessening his value as a dependable factor in the agricultural development of the islands.

Education has increased the native's normal disinclination for manual labor, but available clerkships in Honolulu shops and elsewhere in the islands are limited, even though he sought and was invariably competent to fill them. The splendid Kamehameha training-schools, founded and endowed by Bernice Pauahi Bishop, great-grand-daughter of Kamehameha the Great, are expected to afford much relief in this direction by fitting the native for the trades, which attract him more than the unskilled toil of the fields.

The lower-class native shuns the field as the owl does the light of day. When he must work he seeks employment on the docks, or preferably on the steamers, where the periods of utmost endeavor at the landings, followed by periods of loafing and singing and smoking while the boat steams from port to port, suit his nature perfectly. And he is a good sailor, too. He works hard and diligently, and handles the boats about the ragged coasts of the islands, and loads and unloads these small steamers in the rough, open waterways, with greater skill than I have seen elsewhere in the world. He is, besides, a strong and masterful swimmer.

Few Hawaiians as yet have sought professional careers, although one or two at Honolulu are lawyers, and the Speaker of the House in 1894 was a native. The majority of the educated ones seek clerkships. Few as yet go into the trades, although some excellent carpenter-work is to be seen at the Kamehameha school-shop. But, in truth, the native, with few exceptions, is stirred to labor only by necessity, and only a very small percentage fit themselves for

LAU'IALO GROVE, HAWAII

the higher positions of mercantile houses or for the more skill-requiring trades. In the ordinary course of daily work the native cannot, in point of fact, compete with the Chinamen, who substantially fill the majority of places in the machine, carpenter, and other shops where expert work is requisite, and leave few vacancies in fields of labor less exacting.

And the Chinaman carries his competition further, and with as great success—he very nearly monopolizes the lower class of Hawaiian women.

"John," as those who have come in contact with him know, is the very quintessence of industry. He is the only man in the Far East who continues working after he has accumulated a couple of dollars. The Japanese, Siamese, Malay, and the Hawaiian invariably quits work until the last dollar is spent. The Chinaman is a good provider, and kind to the weaker members of his household; so in Hawaii, as in Siam, the native woman marries him in preference to her own countryman.

Some curious variations of types result from these crossings. In Siam the individuality of the Chinaman is strongly stamped on his progeny, which, although called a Simo-Chinese, is in disposition and appearance a Chinaman. In Hawaii, Chinese blood crossed with native produces a much lighter complexion than is common to either parent, and, on occasions, curly hair, which neither father nor mother ever had. Not many native women marry Portuguese, who view their womankind as working partners seven days of the week, and practically none marry the Japanese, who are not favorably regarded as husbands, however much their progressive spirit may be admired.

So plain John Chinaman, cast out of many lands and a drudge in many others, yet wins his way by very force of his indefatigable industry, marvellous patience, love of children, and his business integrity. In very truth he is the one indispensable factor in Far-Eastern trade—the industrial backbone of Siam, the pioneer of Malayan development, the financier of Japan.

It is one of the remarkable exhibits of this century that the Chinaman should be so invaluable in the development and progress of other countries, while his own land—the prey of Europe—carries the impress of the Dark Ages, unenlightened by contact with the world, and steeped in corruption—political jobbery—of a character so widespread, so infamous, as to continue unrivalled even in the new world.

The Hawaiian woman of the better class marries her countryman, or preferably a white man—just now the American more generally. As a rule she is more amenable to foreign surroundings than the native man, and more quickly adjusts herself to the changing relations. While in her ignorant state, and married to a native, she is apt to be easy of virtue and careless of environment—educated, and the wife of a white man, she becomes the affectionate mother of his children, the wife with an eye single to his interests, and a well-defined idea of her worldly position. In fact, she is exceedingly jealous of her wifely rights.

The children of these marriages between white men and native women —and it is to the credit of the country, and to the lessons taught so long and so persistently by the missionaries, that there are marriages—are destined to be among the most useful citizens of Hawaii. Here again results in these mid-Pacific islands differ materially from those in the countries on the farther side of the Pacific. The Eurasian (compound of Europe and Asia), as the child of a white father and an Asian mother is called in the Far East, seems to inherit the better qualities of neither parent. As a rule, if he is not irresponsible, he is an inconsequential member of society, easily swayed by pleasure, and with no thought of the morrow. The half caste girls are always an improvement, in looks, on their

CARVED FEMALE FIGURE FOR SEAT

mothers, and some are comparatively attractive; but the boys are slight of figure and delicate of constitution—and both are warm of temperament and yielding.

In the Far East there is no mingling of white man and half-caste, except in the relation of employer and employee, or at a time and in a place where the white man's friends will not look for him. Speaking generally, though of course there are exceptions to every rule, a Eurasian very rarely enters the society of the white residents, and the exceptional occasions are when the parentage on one side or the other has been distinguished.

In the Hawaiian Islands there is literally no race distinction whatever, no matter what the cross—and there are some extraordinary combinations. At the President's garden fête may be seen half whites, half Chinese and Hawaiian, Chinese-Hawaiian-German, and though the ancestors on the Chinese or native side, and in some instances on the white side too, may have been lacking in education and refinement, as we understand it, yet the results are pleasing to the eye and gratifying as to intellect. Teachers at schools I visited told me that the child of Hawaiian-Chinese parentage was bright and apt and diligent, while the half white appears to combine some of the enterprise and practicability of his father with the dark eyes and poetic temperament of his mother. White girls

A PRIMITIVE NATIVE HOUSE

THE PASSING NATIVE

never have married full-blooded natives—at least I heard of none who had—but white girls occasionally marry half whites among the educated classes—and I may add in passing that there are no marriages these days with white blood, in the smallest quantity, where there is not education—and the instances of white men marrying half-white girls are very frequent and happy. The half-white girl is quite the most attractive (human) feature of the islands.

In this way there is to be the true fusion of interests and peoples that will one day make of Hawaii the happiest, most truly prosperous land on the face of the globe.

But the native, pure and simple, is passing. Yes, and so fulfilling the unbending laws of nature. His decrease has been startlingly large and rapid (from 108,579 in 1836 to 39,504 in 1896), because he himself has abetted it by a fatalism and an early, persistent debauchery more pronounced than revealed perhaps by any other people in modern history.

Like all aborigines, the Hawaiians are peculiarly susceptible to contagion, and, like many, utterly unmindful of the commonest laws of hygiene. They appear never to have been a race of either marked vitality or industry, and there has been too much coddling of them by the resident whites to breed either quality in the present generation of the full-blooded native. In 1848 one-fourth of the population died of measles; shortly afterwards another 3000 died of small-pox, while the venereal diseases originally taken from the sailors of visiting foreign ships spread, because of the early and protracted licentiousness, throughout all the islands, resulting at length in a large average of genital impotency.

This is one of the reasons, perhaps the principal one, why the native is passing.

Continuous laborious effort of the missionaries early attacked lustful desires and stayed the ravages of their accompanying disease, but the seeds had been sown widely, and are bearing fruit even to-day, though in an infinitely less degree.

There is some improvement in the observance of hygienic laws by Hawaiians, but usually the native pays little attention to rules or regulations governing or preserving health. The native, and more particularly the one in the country, lives about as he has from time long past. He is cleanly as to person but dirty as to surroundings, and though the unhealthful grass house is vanishing, fever and bowel complaints, typhoid and pneumonia, are highly fatal to him, and seize upon him much more frequently than upon his white or half-white neighbors. It is not that disease attacks the native with greater violence; it is that he appears to have less vitality, by no means to be attributed to his surroundings, but to his inheritance of a vitiated blood; for the whites and half whites and all other races thrive healthfully everywhere on the islands, with their trade-winds and wholesome subsoil.

The same inheritance is answerable for his being the more frequent sufferer from leprosy, that dread malady whose charnel-house is on the island of Molokai, and whose victims live there as dead to the world as those under the ground. A vigilant health board and the gradual purging of the old native stock by death or by cleaner living are having happy results in this direction, and leprosy is diminishing, slowly but really. At the time of my visit (September, 1898) the last record showed nearly 1200 on Molokai, of which 984 were natives, 62 half-castes, 32 Chinese, and 5 Americans. Whites contract leprosy but rarely, and then only by inoculation. But so does this disease defy all rules in attack and development that it comes now swiftly and without pain, again slowly and with great pain; a leprous woman may bear a healthful, untainted child; or the taint may reveal itself in the tender years of a child born of apparently healthful, non-leprous father and mother. There are homes for non-leprous boys and for girls born of leprous parents. Careful surveillance of the islands and im-

IDOL

mediate isolation of the patients seem to be successfully holding this terrible disease in check, and time may root it out entirely.

Such has been the magnificent work of Hawaii's Board of Health.

But not all the vigilance of the government has been able to abolish *Kahuna* practice, although it has been materially and generally abated, and especially in Honolulu, which is equal to saying Oahu—for Honolulu is Oahu.

The *Kahuna* is the prototype of the white man's faith-cure doctor, only the Hawaiian has less intelligence to oppose him, and is therefore the more successful of the two quacks. Moreover, his talents are more various and more entertaining. Sometimes he is a soothsayer, and not infrequently a minstrel, and always he is more fanciful, which is in keeping with the claptrap of his profession. His medical theory is simple, and has the very excellent and unique quality of inexpense — to the patient. Most of the prescriptions are administered vicariously — to the ailing man's relatives — and as the nostrums consist very considerably of roasted pig and the favorite native intoxicant *awa*, the popularity of the *Kahuna* may be surmised.

The relatives, being feasted, set up a musical chant, while the fakir doses the patient with broth of herbs or leaves, or hangs a talisman about his neck, or perhaps does all these — if the pig has been particularly toothsome. In the old days the

ON THE ROAD TO WAIKIKI

THE PASSING NATIVE

Kahuna was the priest of the land, a hereditary and greatly revered class, who not infrequently aided the people in their troubles with oppressive chiefs. His outward and visible sign is—or rather was, because now he is an outlaw—a scarlet handkerchief worn about the neck, and the day is not long gone when the sight of him on the road caused bowed head and bended knee. Fear of the law now robs him of obeisance.

You may inquire for *Kahunas*, as I did, at many native houses on the several islands of the Hawaiian group, and be told that faith has departed, and the whereabouts of none is known; but let a member of that same family fall ill, and the *Kahuna* will be sent for first, and the doctor second — the native to receive the credit of a cure, the doctor the opprobrium of a death.

And that is another reason why the native is passing.

There are excellent qualities in the native, as the blood reveals upon its mixture with other and stronger races, but unadulterated he is not equal to filling an active place in the progress overtaking his land. The Hawaiians are a polite, easy-going people, sensitive to ridicule and criticism, and flowery of speech; indolent, cheerful, generous, and honest. Children they are really, with an inordinate fondness for flattery, and other sweets more material. In appearance there is unmistakable Polynesian resemblance, with overfulness of lips and broadness of nose, though their skin is never so dark as the negro's. They have small feet, a deliberate, upright gait, and the women have taper fingers, and a peculiar swinging motion of the hip at each step to which the shoulder responds. They have no word to express thanks, or chastity, or gratitude, or the weather; but they love flowers, music — surely what sweeter, purer things could they love? — and their native songs are full of melody and sentiment. In play they are delightful; in living, Arcadian; in work they labor under the disadvantage that comes to all children of nature. You pity their improvidence, and perhaps their irresponsibility may irritate, but the gentle, affectionate nature of these soft-voiced people must appeal to your heart.

Improvidence and indolence are by no means traits of modern development. 'Twas always so. I have before me the report of a board appointed in 1843 to seek the best means of "abolishing indolence and indifference, and introducing habits of general industry, continuously pursued." In those days the common laborer was paid from twelve to twenty-five cents a day; the carpenter, from twenty-five to seventy-five cents; the farm-hand, from four to five dollars a month. To-day the common laborer earns from seventy-five cents to one dollar a day, the carpenter from two to three and one-half dollars; the farm-hand from twenty to thirty dollars a month, and the house-servant from four to five dollars a week. Chinese and Japanese are the house servants of Hawaii, the natives being not inclined to domestic service, and, indeed, even in the most humble circumstances, are employers. Apparently no native home is too lowly to have its own servant.

The cost of their living has of necessity advanced very little, but their habits have increased in expense. In the old days they used to grow and catch their food; now the Chinese cultivate the *taro* and make the *poi*, and catch most of the fish to sell to the native, who works for wages when he must, and plays when he may.

And so, with the flower *leis* about his hat, and the light of contentment in his eye, the native Hawaiian is passing—blending with the stronger race for the making of a composite type—unique, attractive, alert—more fitted to combat with nineteenth-century civilization and life.

Meanwhile, during the evolution, he is better paid, better housed and clothed, is freer, and has more voice in the government of his country and of himself.

CHAPTER V

FROM OAHU TO HAWAII

ALL Hawaii centres around Honolulu; therefore it is fitting we begin our tour of the islands at Oahu—of which, however, I have already written so much that little remains to be added.

The Hawaiian group, including a chain of coral islets reaching into the northwest, numbers about twenty islands—all of volcanic origin—the principal inhabited ones being, in order of size, Hawaii, Maui, Oahu, Kauai, Molokai, Lanai, Niihau, and Kahoolawe; the smaller and uninhabited, Molokini, Lehua, Kanla, Bird, Necker, and about ten others.

As I have said, Oahu, in my judgment, is the most attractive of them all, the peculiarity of its beauty being verdant hills rising abruptly out of fields of taro and rice, to end in minarets and domes of gray rock veiled ever now and again by the always moving clouds of multiple shadings.

But you may see all of Oahu that is worth viewing by short excursions from Honolulu, and you will find nothing novel aside from the scenery.

There is little left of native life; the island is completely Americanized.

With exception of the sterile soil around the several points, Oahu is one great sugar plantation, though desirable ground on the northeast side is scarce, with patches of rice and taro here and there on the very fertile wet lowlands. To no one man is this extensive cane growing so much due as to Benjamin F. Dillingham, whose unshaken faith in the possibilities of the island and undaunted enterprise built the railroad which permitted cultivation of land otherwise unprofitable for planting. It is not saying too much to declare that the railroad, tapping as it does all the sugar land, has been the making of industrial Oahu.

In the centre of the island are some 60,000 acres of pasture-land, not sufficiently rich for sugar, but possibly good enough for farming under irrigation—and nowhere is there land not already owned or under long lease.

Oahu is no island for the immigrant.

You may have the choice of two routes to the island of Hawaii, but only one company owns the steamers — which, by-the-way, is one of Hawaii's chief grievances and most certain handicaps to industrial development.

I chose to make my first landing on the leeward or dry side of the island, and set sail from Honolulu at ten o'clock in the morning on the *Kinau*, a propeller of about nine hundred tons, with clean, com-

HAWAIIAN-AMERICA

fortable cabins and a general trig appearance. Passing close to Diamond Head on the southeast end of Oahu, we had a satisfying view of this famous

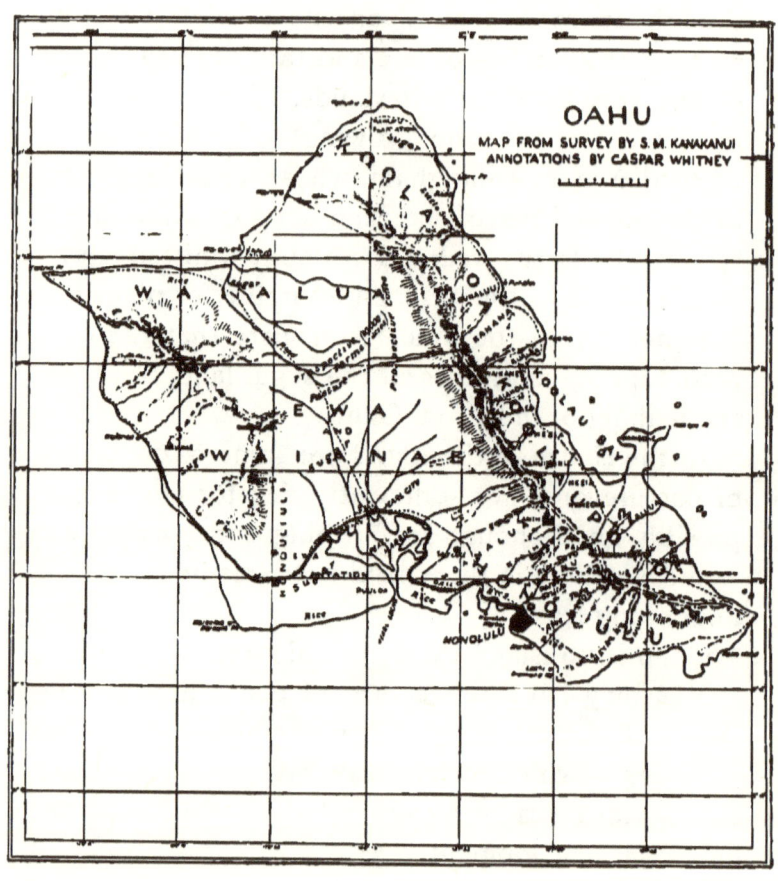

extinct crater — a veritable bowl, with edges so narrow one can barely circle its very rim on foot.

Shortly we were crossing the (30) miles of Kaiwi

Channel, which was rather rough, as most of the Hawaiian channels are, and soon came off the south (leeward) side of Molokai, the island home of the lepers. The west end of the island, where herds of the little Chinese spotted-deer and some cattle and horses seem to thrive on the dry grass, looks a dreary waste and is treeless and mountainless, although leased by an American company, which is beginning to plant in cane some of the southerly sections. We could see them working where a sugar-plantation is starting, and the soil appeared rich and red; it is claimed enough water can be obtained from wells sunk near the sea, thus catching the rain which drains from the back country. There is no other available water here; little, indeed, from any source on the south side, and hanging fortune and hope on so slim and uncertain a supply seems risky. But the very rich soil is too tempting.

Far back could be seen the precipice which shuts off the lepers from the other inhabitants of Molokai.

To the east of the plantation the steamer stopped off a little fringe of cocoanut-trees and a few houses, which together make the settlement of Kaunakaka, to pick up some native passengers who were rowing out to us.

A few fields of taro seemed all the agricultural industry in sight. Beyond, the bare, sterile hills rise abruptly from the shore, and except for one little spot farther on, where a rift has permitted the escape of some good soil, there is no place where a living thing thrives. The one live little spot is Kanolo, where some rice and taro are growing, and a church stands square and solemn and white against a rugged grayish background. East-

REMAINS OF AN ANCIENT HEIAU, OR TEMPLE OF REFUGE, NEAR KAWAIHAE, HAWAII

(Built by Kamehameha the Great)

ward from here the mountains come down to the water, with only two short stretches where foothold may be secured, so to say, until the high point, the extreme eastern point, of Molokai is rounded.

FROM OAHU TO HAWAII

The north or windward side of the island, with a few small fertile valleys, is as bright and fresh-looking as the south side is barren.

Crossing Pailolo into Auau Channel, we arrived off Lahaina (Maui) about four in the afternoon, having viewed the small barren island of Lanai, which is given up entirely to sheep, except for a small bit on the northeast side, where a sugar-plantation, depending on wells, is about to be started.

Maui is second in size to Hawaii, and consists of two mountains split into deep, beautiful valleys. East Maui is much the bigger half of the island, and, besides having Haleakala, the largest known crater in the world (height, 10,000 feet; depth, 2000 feet; length, $7\frac{1}{2}$ miles; circumference, 20 miles), has quite the greater share of arable land. And all that is available for cultivation is already under lease. West Maui's chief attraction is its scenery, with its steeper mountains and more picturesque valleys. There are no immediate opportunities for settlers on this island; the land not in use is sterile, and the soil at best is expensive to cultivate, because irrigation is almost invariably needful.

The two settlements of importance are Wailuku, on the windward or north side, and Lahaina, on the leeward side of the neck of land that connects the east and west halves of the island. Wailuku's chief claim to distinction rests in its being the centre of Maui sugar-planting interests and the starting-point of a railroad that runs back a dozen miles towards the mountains and the sugar-mills. It has a court-house, several shops and churches, and an exalted opinion of itself.

Lahaina is a relic of departed glory. It was a famous town in ancient days—a commercial centre when the whaling interests flourished, the residence of kings — the chief city, in fact, of all Hawaii. But all the old buildings have gone, and there remains nothing now to suggest one-time importance. It is a sleepy little port—a restful, mildly tempered haven for invalids. The best idea of industrial Maui can be gained from the map appended, upon which I have made copious annotations.

From Lahaina to Maalaea Bay is a couple of hours' steaming; but there is no settlement here, and the port exists chiefly as the landing-place on this side of the island for Wailuku on the north side. There are no docks at any of these ports, and no harbors. The steamers lie out in an

A BIT OF THE NEW GOVERNMENT ROAD TO HILO

open roadway, often quite rough; and passengers and freight are rowed ashore by natives, who are expert water-men, and take the boats through the heavy choppy seas, in and out of the jagged, half-moon indentations that answer for harbors, with exceeding skill.

It is a rough-and-tumble trip across the Hawaii Channel from Makena (Maui) to Kawaihae (Hawaii), and therefore you do not mind the unseemly hour of arrival (2.30 A.M.), but until daylight comes to reveal the unattractiveness of its environment, you wonder at the number of people assembled on the landing at such an hour. You understand later. Once, many years ago, Kawaihae was a thriving port, where the whalers came for the potatoes raised on the hills directly back of the settlement, and people lived here and prospered. Now the settlement owes its life to the weekly arrival of the steamer from Honolulu. Small wonder its handful of residents shake off sleep to view this periodical deliverance from utter stagnation!

Kawaihae is a bite out of the coast, with high rocky hills standing immediately back of the bay, and a narrow shore-line fringed with cocoa-palms and algaroba-trees. The algaroba is the mesquite of Mexico and Arizona, whose large, sweet, and fleshy pods provide the most fattening fodder for cattle and horses, but it does not grow above an elevation of 300 feet in Hawaii, and therein differs from the mesquite of our Southwest. The cocoa-palm is to the Hawaiian what the caribou is to the Northwest Indians — it furnishes milk, oil, food, rope, matting, and each tree produces about one hundred nuts annually. It is, besides, the one most pleasing object in all the islands, with its rakish beauty and long, slender, wrinkled trunks crowned with a top of feathery leaves.

Kawaihae's one remaining point of interest is the ruins on the hill of a temple of refuge built by Kamehameha the Great. It is the very last of the Heiaus, where in the old days, during strife, the peaceful sought and obtained immunity from harm—for into these temples a man might not pursue an enemy. This ruin indicates a very substantial structure, in parallelogram form, about 220 feet long by 100 feet wide. Entrance is gained through a narrow passage between two high walls, and the interior is laid off in terraces and paved with smooth flat stones. The wall uphill is 8 feet high, and on the downhill side 20 feet high, and both are 12 feet thick at base.

It was my good fortune that W. G. Irwin, one of the leading men of affairs in the islands, and Samuel Parker, a descendant of native nobility, and Minister of Foreign Affairs under the monarchy (Liliuokalani), had also been on the *Kinau*, the former bent on a tour of his plantations, the latter returning to his cattle-ranch home at Mana.

So we sat together under the trees until daylight, and then started for the house of Paul Jarrett, man-

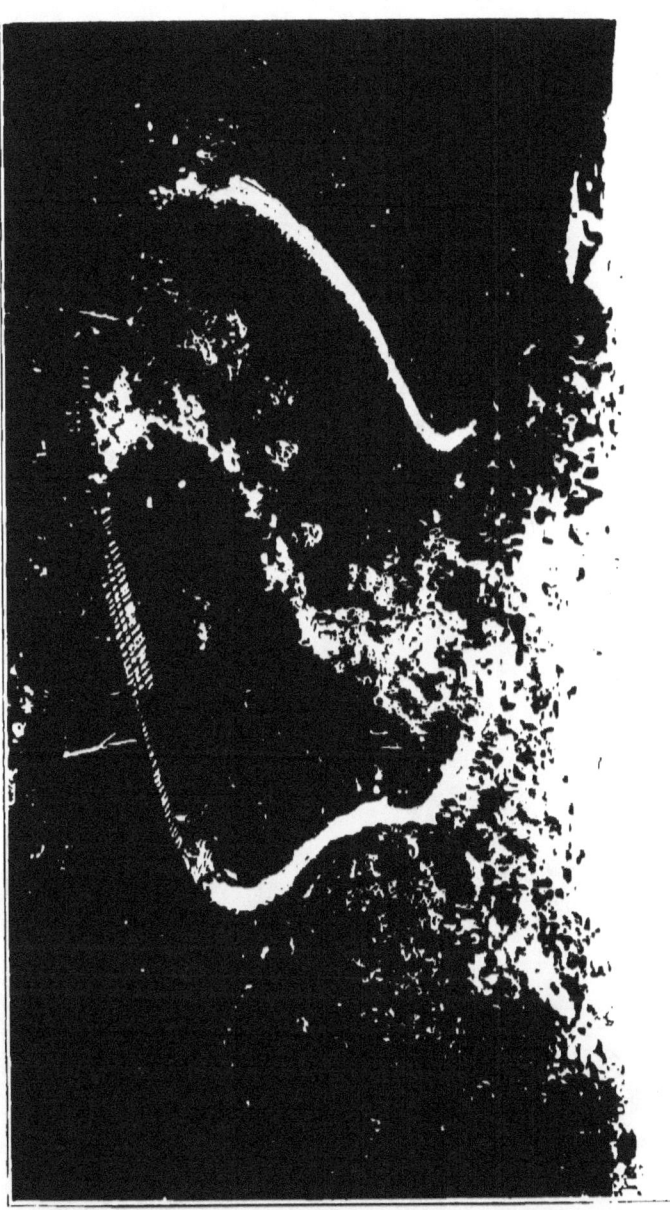

SUGAR PLANTATION AND THE OAHU RAILROAD

ager for Mr. Parker, at Waimea. As we toiled up from the water's edge, a beautiful view was disclosed of Hawaii's three great mountains — Mauna Kea (13,805 feet), Mauna Loa (13,675 feet), and Hualalai (8275 feet).

Waimea is thirteen miles from Kawaihae, and the road in that distance climbs 2700 feet through a rocky, barren country that seems fit for nothing but goats and sisal. But as you approach Waimea, the rocks disappear and the country opens out into a valley about five to seven miles wide, which extends for fifteen miles, until it runs down to the sea above Honokoa on the north side of the island. There is no running water on this tract, and practically no trees until half of its length has been traversed, except where it touches on either side the edges of the mountain forest which are receding so rapidly.

It is a pleasing country, this valley, covered with quantities of nourishing *manieni* (Bermuda) and Hilo grass, and broken into numberless knolls and swales that afford shelter from strong and constant winds. Unluckily the Hilo grass (introduced by a doctor of Hilo only twenty-three years ago, and now spread over all the islands) is crowding out the Bermuda, which is much the thicker and more nutritious, and was brought to Hawaii from South America.

En route to Mana we fell in with the school-master for that district, who, in addition to tilling the young mind, maintains a truck-farm and a dairy, and is the government assessor as well. He was quite the most enthusiastic granger I encountered. He placed no limit on the agricultural possibilities of Hawaii, and was as ready to practically illustrate the fruit-canning prospects as he was to dig potatoes to convince me of their average size and the number to

HALF WHITE HULA-HULA DANCER AND (NOSE) FLUTE-PLAYER

the hill. We side-tracked to have a look at his little farm, where he had growing strawberries, cucumbers, asparagus, cauliflower, cabbage, onions, tomatoes—though none properly cared for, and therefore not looking very well. There was also a small patch of corn, of no cheerful appearance. He told

us he had raised some wheat hay the previous year and disposed of it with profit—hay usually is imported and costs $30 on these islands—and claimed also to get eighty pounds of butter a week from thirty cows — fed once a day on corn-stalks, and given no middlings—which he sells for 50 cents per pound.

Having discoursed glowingly on Hawaii's great opportunity to supply California with fruit in its between season, and dug up some fine large potatoes, for which he assured us he got $1 per bag of one hundred pounds, this pedagogic jack-of-all-trades retired within his house and proceeded to serenade us with cornet and piano—relying on the former and his right hand to carry the air, while his left did chord duty on the piano. Later he shot some plover, which we ate next morning, and found fat and excellent.

While this man has made no especial agricultural success, at least what he has accomplished suggests the capabilities of the soil under intelligent cultivation. Just at the time of our visit he was making and canning guava jelly, and as the fruit grows wild everywhere on the island, there would seem to be some money in the venture.

This entire tract from Waimea running north, controlled by the Parkers, includes six to seven hundred thousand acres, of which about two hundred and fifty to three hundred thousand is excellent land, and, under irrigation, fit to raise anything.

HAWAIIAN-AMERICA

At present it is an ideal cattle-ranch, with water piped from the mountains into drinking-tanks. Parker has about thirty thousand head of cattle, and owns about one-third of this immense tract; the balance he has on lease, which expires in 1913, and, as it is the finest land of its kind on the island, its market value will probably be greatly increased. In return for extension of his lease in the last days of the monarchy, Parker gave up one thousand acres in the centre of this valley tract to the government, for the making of twenty-five acre homesteads. Riding through these small homesteads, which are on either side the main road, one sees what care and water can do in the way of producing flowers and garden truck. Speaking generally, although the rain is uncertain, there is enough for crops in this district. The country was very dry on my visit, and from what I heard and saw I judge the condition was not unusual.

A worm peculiar to all these islands is deadly to vegetation, and must be destroyed before certain crops can be depended on. The Japanese beetle also is destructive to flowers and plants of all kinds. There are some peach and orange trees, but neither seem to flourish in this particular locality. Bananas and figs could be raised lower down. Mangoes, alligator-pears, bread-fruit are to be found, but it is really astonishing how little fruit there is, considering the quality of the soil. And the same comment is true of vegetables; all kinds can be grown, yet rice and taro only are produced in abundance.

The school-master thought wheat could be raised, and there is no doubt of it, up to the limit of local consumption, but not beyond it, in either sufficient quality or quantity.

WAIPIO VALLEY, HUNINI

The noticeable features of this part of Hawaii are the rapidly receding forests and the treeless valleys. It has come to pass that one must ride deep into the forest to get beyond the belt of dying timber. Cattle, it is said, are responsible for this denudation, and perhaps their trampling of the tender roots does in part account for it; but it seems more likely the roots strike rock and die for lack of nourishing soil and rain.

There are now only left in abundance the *ohia*— the native apple-tree, with gaudy crimson blossom and somewhat tasteless fruit—the tree which furnishes the *lehua* flower, dear to poetical Hawaii —and the magnificent tree-ferns that stand so high as twenty-five feet. The *mamani*—a wood so hard that fence-posts of it last six years—is also disappearing, and, indeed, the forest in this section seems to be composed principally of *ohia*, tree-ferns and creepers, and underbrush. The creepers are in greatest profusion, varying in size of stem from whip-cord to a man's arm, and climbing over and entangling the tallest trees.

Mana is the most entrancing spot I found in all Hawaii, deeply comforting after a day in the saddle. It is the soft-toned name by which the immediate site of Mr. Parker's ranch home (3500 feet elevation) is known, and a little care and much water—rain in sufficient quantity being lacking— have made of it a veritable flower-garden. A rambling old house of one story has been enlarged from time to time until now two wings run out at right angles, quite the length of the original home. Honeysuckle, under a row of Norfolk pines, assails your nostrils at the rear of the house, and at the front the deliciously balmy air is heavy with heliotrope. There are daisies (which cannot be

COFFEE IN OHIA FOREST, HAWAII—THE FAMOUS HAWAIIAN FERN-TREE IN THE FOREGROUND

raised at Honolulu), pansies, roses, hydrangeas, and clumps of ironwood-trees, with their dainty feathery branches traced against the sky—also the eucalyptus, and a tree quite like the California redwood, all imported and flourishing.

Next morning, before setting out for a cattle round-up, our hats and necks were encircled, as the pretty custom of the country is, with *leis* made from the plentiful and sweet-smelling flowers of Mana.

There are considerable numbers of wild cattle and wild pig in Hawaii—*i. e.*, the domestic variety gone wild after years of running loose in the mountains — and at every round-up for branding there is a considerable haul of mavericks. We rode across the hills and for six miles through the dead timber that lay thick in desolate array before we came to the live forest, and eventually to where Jarrett had corralled about thirteen hundred head of cattle. Both native cattle and horses are smaller, and somewhat weedier than our Western species, but all looked in very fair condition, which speaks rather well for Hilo grass—the only kind found deep in the forest.

Weediness in cattle however would prevent this country from putting native butter into open market competiton until a much better breed had been introduced.

From the cattle-pen, where there was ample evidence of excellent native cowboy work, we rode through the forest, across the mountains,

HAWAIIAN-AMERICA

and towards the sea, where the forest ceases and the upland is considered coffee land, down into the Paauhau sugar-plantation's uppermost fields (1700 feet elevation), where the cane was too dry to look well. For several miles we rode through field after field, the cane waving above one's head and shutting out view of everything save the water at the foot of the slope we were descending. Eventually we reached the house of Mr. Irwin's manager, Mr. Moore, where we were all put up for the night. The hospitality that greets the traveller in these Hawaiian Islands is as generous as it is spontaneous and graciously offered.

The great business of running a sugar-plantation must be studied to be fully appreciated; there are railroads with cars and engines, and flumes and trestles over one hundred feet high and thousands of feet long, to carry the cane from the field to the mill; there are cables and cars and engines to put it on ship, and landing-places, merely for plantation use, that cost $30,000. The Paauhau mill has a capacity of sixty tons of sugar a day, and cost $250,000, but there are some, a great deal larger, and costing twice that amount.

Apropos of Hawaii's "legalized slavery"—which I discuss in another chapter—I talked with one Japanese sugar-boiler in the Paauhau mill who had saved over $3000!

This, the windward side of the island, differs very materially from the other in appearance, being

TRESTLE 120 FEET HIGH, TO CARRY CANE FLUME ACROSS GULCH ON PLANTATION ON HAWAII

greener and therefore brighter and more fertile. From the two noble mountains, Mauna Kea and Mauna Loa, whose rise is so gentle it is difficult to realize their great height, the country descends quite abruptly to about six to seven thousand feet elevation, then with an open strip, followed by forest, it comes down with a gradual slope, broken by innumerable gulches, until it terminates at the sea in a bluff that may be from fifty to three hundred feet in height. The map gives no idea whatever of the broken shore-line—it is a succession of deep indentations and sharp protruding tongues of rock. In the final thirty miles from Laupahoehoe to Hilo there are 65 gulches, from 125 to 750 feet deep, each with water, each beautiful in the wild vagaries of tropical verdure. I know them—every one—I had my bicycle with me.

To any one with an idea of touring the island of Hawaii on a bicycle, I beg to offer an earnest—don't. I took a bicycle with me to save time. I had not before ridden over the roads of Hawaii, nor could I find any one who had—on a bicycle. I had wished to reach Hilo, about fifty-six miles, the night of the morning I left Messrs. Irwin, Parker, and Moore at Paauhau, but had not been riding long before I realized the futility of such a hope. For twenty miles the road is fairly good, except that the hills are too steep to ride either up or down in comfort, and the road is always running up or down hill.

The character of the country remains practically the same along this entire coast — cane-fields on both sides of the road down to the bluff at the water's edge, and up, high as the eye reaches above the sugar belt, is the coffee, and above that again pasture. My map goes into these details very carefully. There is quite a little coffee-growing industry at Ookala and other near-by sections, where the Portuguese have taken up land, and the Japanese too have secured some leases. There is no timber anywhere along on the coast in sufficient size to attract a saw-mill.

Laupahoehoe, where I lunched, is a long, deep gulch, filled with earth and rock instead of water, and at its outermost edge are a dozen houses, a church, and a few cocoanut-palms. From here to Hakalau, fourteen miles, there is only a trail, which —regardless of grade— plunges straight down to the bottom of every gulch, and rises again equally as straight on the opposite side. Throughout the fourteen miles there is hardly enough level road to give it name—you pick your way down into one gulch, only to struggle out and immediately dive into another. One gulch, Maulau, is 500 feet deep, and occupied me one hour in crossing. I could not roll my wheel—I had practically to keep pushing it above me as I climbed up, and dropping it below me as I scrambled down. And when I reached the prettily located house of Mr. George Ross, long after dark, I was about the most torn and bespat-

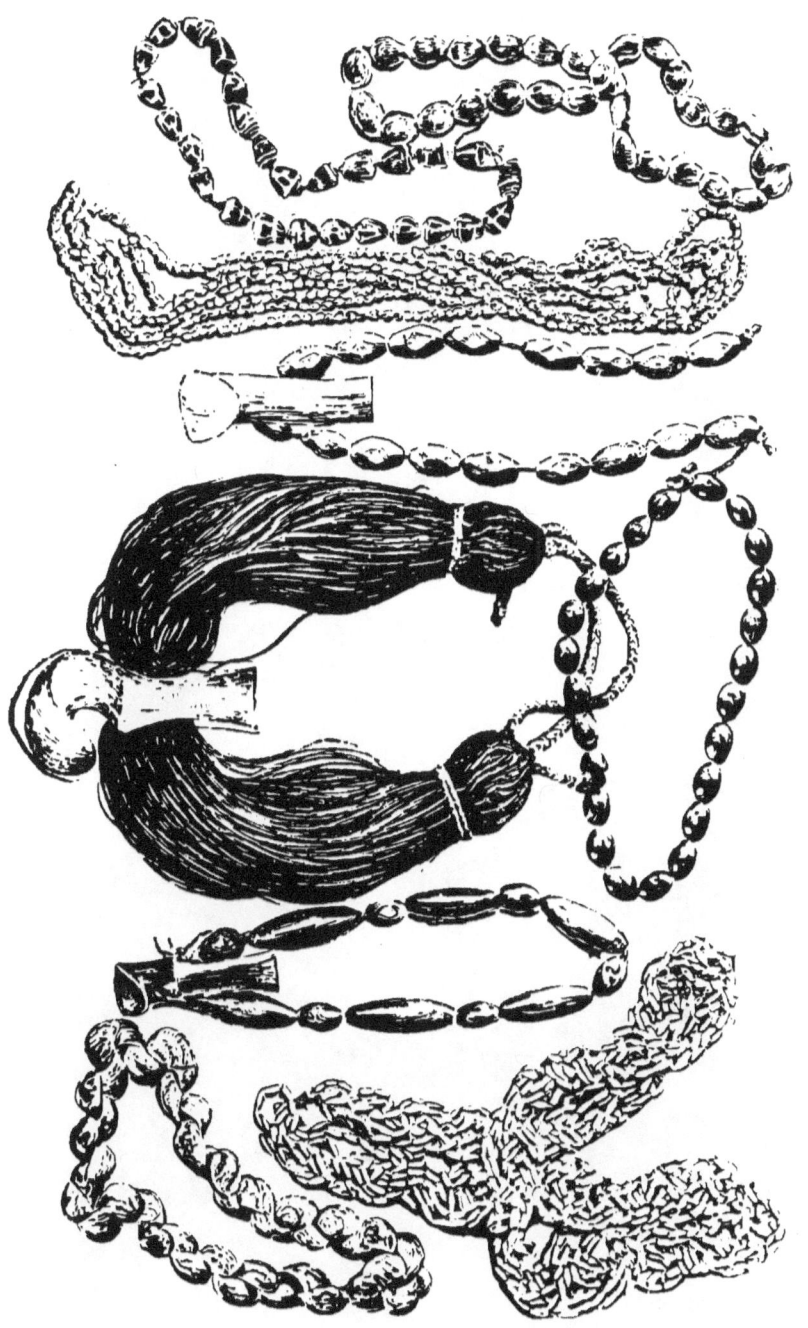

tered creature, I fancy, and perhaps as weary a one, as had ever tramped into Hakalau.

The next day I pursued my trip on to Hilo in a two-wheel cart Mr. Ross was so kind as to loan me, and not again on Hawaii did I undertake bicycling.

The country continues very much broken from Hakalau, but the road is in excellent condition, and a moderate grade is observed in crossing the gulches, which are many and deep. There is such an abundance of water, approaching Hilo, that planters extensively use flumes for conveying the cane to the mill: several times the road passes under high trestles carrying great stretches of fluming across the gulches, and one side hill flume I noted was four miles long.

After its pretty bay—the only possible harbor in all Hawaii besides Honolulu and Pearl harbors—and the picturesque approach, Hilo town is a disappointment. It is built much more like a town on a Kansas plain than one amid the luxuriance of the semi-tropics. Except for one or two attractive bungalows it has the same square, prim houses, with the two main business streets running at right angles and very conventionally filled with shops fashioned after the severe

SLEDGE FOR SLIDING DOWN HILL

architectural lines of northern New England. As at Honolulu, nothing is here to suggest the tropics except the foliage. Hilo has a population of about 13,000, a hotel, electric light, a small wharf, and a prospective trolley-line to the volcano.

WAILUKU, MAUI, ENTRANCE TO FAMOUS IAO VALLEY

During the time of my visit the town was convulsed by views of its expected prosperity—real-estate values inflated, and agents innumerable dealing in coffee futures. It seemed tottering on the verge of a boom, which, I fear, would do it more harm than good. All kinds of rumors were afloat of large investments in coffee-planting, and all kinds of reports rampant as to profits and yield, most of them unreliable and greatly exaggerated. Fancy figures were being asked for land, and unlimited speculation indulged as to prospective yield—matters which experience alone can determine. Considerable harm has already been done the industry by inexperienced men rushing blindly into it and failing. So far as making big money is concerned, the industry is yet experimental, but there are many successes where comparatively small patches have been worked carefully and thoroughly.

From Hilo to the volcano (Kilauea) the road runs through the Olaa and Puna districts, two of Hawaii's most favored coffee-growing localities. This entire section is covered with forest and jungle, and almost all of it carries a deep rich soil of decomposed lava that will produce anything. As usual, the natives neglect their opportunity; not so the Japanese, however, whose vegetable gardens are to be seen in every direction from Hilo. There is surprising scarcity of fruit; one can get more variety, and as cheap, in almost any American seaport. The pressing need of Hawaii is more roads. There is now but the single road around the island, very poor in many parts, and impassable in some. An upper road above the sugar belt, along the windward side, is wanted, also one running parallel with the volcano road, and another one or two at right angles with it into the lands suitable for coffee.

The character of the soil and country changes entirely after passing the volcano and going through Kau district towards Punaluu on the south. The

HILO, AND ITS PRETTY BAY

soil now is sand and reddish dirt, with stifling dust half a foot deep—for here there is no rain. The road winds over and around lava all the way to Pahala, twenty-six miles. Sometimes you travel over solid lava, and again it opens a little, and grass struggles to live here and there in patches. Cattle manage to exist on a ranch crossed midway of the distance, but could not, except that up in the mountains they may get better grass and some water. And this is the general character of the country from the forest edge on Mauna Loa down to the very water.

Pahala is the headquarters for a very large sugar-plantation, which extends along the coast for a number of miles, taking in a good strip of land that is to be found between the lava flow, which runs from the sea-coast inland about three miles, and the forest belt. But above and below and at both sides is lava, which runs straight down to the water's edge, to make a wild-looking coast. This fringe of lava skirts the southern coast from Punaluu east for fifty miles, and west and north of Punaluu to Hookena.

Punaluu is quite the most desolate-looking place I beheld, with its handful of houses set upon bare, black lava banks, a solitary, prim little church, and angry waves lashing themselves into foam against the broken shore-line. Though the scene is even more cheerless farther along towards the north-west. From the southerly point of Hawaii to Hoopuloa there is nothing but lava, sometimes in benches, generally, however, in one continuous slope, running down to the sea, with no vegetation visible, though forest may be seen far back upon the mountain. But immediately before you is everywhere lava and a shore-line jagged and fantastic.

Passing Hoopuloa, which is nearly as dreary looking as Punaluu, the predominance of lava lessens, and occasional coffee in patches here and there is seen, until we reach Hookena, a cheerier-looking place on a low piece of land, which seems to be especially bright against the black lava surroundings. It is a fertile little tongue of land, with a cocoanut grove and a half dozen clean-appearing houses.

Now we are in the famous Kona section, where coffee was first grown and more natives of pure blood are yet to be found than in any other island district. The country steadily improves from here, showing occasional strips of lava, but in the main is a great rolling hill-side—devoted to coffee and pasture—running back gradually until at the very top, where it rises more steeply for about three miles to four, and is covered with some forest, and in places discloses the rich soil found wherever volcanic matter has decomposed.

Farther on, Kealakekua Bay is a rather pretty, wedge-shaped inlet—the right arm, a high, sheer bluff (200 feet), which, at its outer end, slopes down to a low, broad, flat point. Just where the flat reaches up to join the bluff are a few houses, a grove of spreading trees, and Captain Cook's monument. The other arm of the bay is lowland edged with lava, with twenty scattering houses, and two groves of cocoanut-trees. A church stands higher up on the hill-side.

But the prettiest place, the only attractive one on the lee coast, is Kailua, the old-time residence of kings, on a small, crescent-shaped bay. The country slopes straight back for three miles to the forest, and the hill-side is dotted with coffee

WINDWARD COAST, HAWAII

and houses. It used to be a very populous district, and remains now the most populous on the island—indeed, I believe it is the only one in all Hawaii where the natives are increasing a little; elsewhere there are three deaths to one birth. Kailua is quite a cattle-shipping point also, and I was much interested in the native manner of loading; the cattle are swum out to the steamer's small boats, and roped by their horns to the oars stretched across the gunwale. The small boats are then hauled to the steamer, each with eight swimming cattle, which are hoisted by a belly-band to the steamer-deck. It is the most humane method I have seen where cattle are not loaded from the wharf immediately into the ship.

I embarked here for Honolulu, and with me quite a number of native travellers whom it is always easy to distinguish by the simple tender custom that prompts their friends to hang *leis* about their necks and around their hats.

Good-natured, easy-going people that they are! it takes very little to give them happiness.

CHAPTER VI

KAUAI—"THE GARDEN ISLAND"

I MADE my landing on Kauai at Nawiliwili, a very pretty crescent-shaped bay with high bold land at the points, disembarking from a smaller steamer than those running to Hawaii and Maui, after one of the roughest trips in my ocean-travelling experience. This channel between Oahu and Kauai is justly far famed for its turbulence. It has several different kinds of concentric and other motions operated simultaneously.

Hawaiians call Kauai the Garden Island of the group — and in so doing raise expectations at Honolulu which will not be realized by a trip across the disturbing channel. It is the oldest of the islands—and therefore freer of lava—but it is also the least picturesque and, I must add, has the least agricultural possibilities for immigrants.

In point of fact, there are no possibilities at all. Not for lack of arable land, indeed, but for lack of any kind worth cultivating. The island is practically owned by about six plantations, and has never been surveyed in whole by the government.

KAUAI—"THE GARDEN ISLAND"

Some of these plantations are on very rich soil—and one of them, at Lihue, just inland from Nawiliwili, has stretches that yield nine tons of sugar to the acre; but the majority do not yield more than half that amount. Physically the island is somewhat like the others, save that its centre is occupied by high (3000 feet) table-land densely covered with forest, instead of ragged mountains, and it has in the Hanalei and Wailua rivers two streams of very fair size.

From Lihue the road goes east over a rolling pasture country, through a gap in the mountains, where rain is always sure to catch you, until it comes to Koloa, where a considerable sugar-plantation is owned by Germans, and managed by a superintendent who wears his mustache like the "mailed fist," and exacts a military salute from his employés. This is the dry side of the island, and here and all along the coast, water for irrigation comes from wells or is piped from the mountains, on which is found the only island timber not even at its largest big enough to furnish lumber. There is not so much lantana on this side the island as on the other, but the Japanese beetle is very active and destroys vegetables, flowers, leaves, and trees. The general character of the country in this section is indeed not unlike some of our Western stretches of grass land, dotted with single widely separated trees and clumps.

Continuing east over more rolling pasture land,

extending from the sea up to the mountains, we cross several small valleys filled with rice-fields, in token of Chinese industry; and wherever there is a valley there also is a little shop kept by a Japanese or a Chinaman. You never see a shop

WAILUA FALLS—KAUAI

kept by natives, and only rarely find them working in the plantation fields. They are not even cultivating their own little patches of taro, as formerly they did, but instead leave all the hard soil-tilling to the Chinamen, and themselves work on

KAUAI—"THE GARDEN ISLAND"

the steamers and docks, where spells of hardest endeavor are followed by periods of entire relaxation. Or they work well about horses, and sometimes at piece-work in the fields, but rarely at daily labor. The native does not mind a scolding, but is very sensitive to ridicule.

The cattle along this section all looked well, although I am told much distress is caused by the horn-fly. At all events, it is a beautiful grazing country hereabouts, until we reach picturesque Hanapepe Valley, eight to nine miles deep, and cultivated for about four miles in rice, which, in various stages of growth, gives beautifully soft shadings to the valley.

The many and sometimes ingenious methods employed by the Chinamen to keep birds from the rice are amusing if not instructive; the common custom is the planting of innumerable little white flags throughout the fields, but there are also windmills working wooden ratchet-wheels, sentinels with guns, and walking women who shout and beat upon empty tin cans.

At Hanapepe Valley the cane-belt begins and runs on past Makaweli and for a few miles beyond Waimea, until there is no cultivation, and only a poor trail leads up over a broken plateau.

The north side of the island is also dry, although water is to be had in the mountains. Except for occasional spots it is an uninteresting country one views riding north from Lihue and then east towards Hanalei. There are stretches of pasture, some very rocky, and now and again a long deep valley filled with rice-fields. Practically no trees are to be seen on the pasture land, though here and there, as a valley is approached, one encounters a bunch of kukui — the tree which supplies the candle-nut formerly burned by the natives in their primitive stone-lamps. These and the hau, too crooked even

ONE OF THE FEW HILO RESIDENCES TO FIT ITS SURROUNDINGS

for firewood but an ideal arbor, and often thickly covered with its brilliant yellow poppies, are, with lantana, the most frequent growth on the rocky pasturage lands.

KAUAI—"THE GARDEN ISLAND"

The plantation settlements against the bare landscape are a relief to the eye, with all their houses cleanly whitewashed, and banana and papaya trees surrounding little patches of cultivation, with once in a while a tiny garden of flowers suggesting an attempt to obtain the color and cheeriness that combine to make habitations home-like.

It was interesting to note the attitude of the different laborers one met in riding over the island. Invariably the native Hawaiians, women and men, looked at us frankly, but friendly and politely, nodding to us in passing; the Portuguese deferentially removed their hats and stopped respectfully until we passed. Not so the Japanese and Chinese: they stared blankly, impassively.

Each little valley is very bright and beautifully green and refreshing, and Hanalei, on a deep bay with high land approaching, is one of the most attractive spots on any of the islands—a cool and picturesque resort. Here the wagon road ends, and a horse-trail continues for twelve miles, when that too ends, and if you wish to circle the island you must climb 800 feet to the top of a cliff, where another trail leads to Waimea.

At the east side of Hanalei Bay the mountains come down to the sea in three sharp ridges; beyond there is only a trail leading over to Kalalau, the only stretch of arable land being in Wainiha Valley, although several little gulches running back from the sea are considered available for coffee.

Hanalei Valley is about ten miles long, and cultivated in rice for three or four miles.

Other than a few little shops to supply local needs at the several small settlements along the

THE FERRY AT HANALEI RIVER

coast, there is no commercial activity on Kauai apart from the sugar industry, which appears to absorb all the enterprise of the island.

For instance, asking for soda-water at the hotel, I was informed that none was to be had, because the man who manufactured it had gone to Honolulu for a few days and locked up his shop. And,

KAUAI—"THE GARDEN ISLAND"

truth to tell, there is no room for enterprise on Kauai. There is no land not already taken up, and none that could be bought. The island is divided into cane, pasture, and valleys. In the latter rice and taro are grown by Chinamen; the cane land is all held by several long-established companies, and the pasture by a few individuals, who have about 20,000 head of cattle and 2000 head of sheep. On

HANALEI VALLEY, KAUAI

the small island of Niihau, which is owned by one family, are other 25,000 sheep.

Cane is planted at an average elevation of 250 feet, though there is some at 500 feet, and yields on the average about five tons of sugar to the acre.

It may be set down as a fact that, under the present exceptionally high price ruling for sugar, all the land available for cane is planted, so there are no possibilities in this direction beyond what are presently realized.

There are, however, coffee-growing possibilities in several of the gulches running back from the sea on the northeast side of the island, especially between Wainiha and Kalalau, where already about 60,000 trees are growing. Kalalau Valley extends four miles, and has some 500 acres of prospective coffee land, held partly on government lease and partly in fee-simple, while there are other 500 acres of coffee land up Wainiha way owned in fee-simple by a company of natives.

Small as is the local demand for fruit and vegetables, not enough of either is grown to supply it; bananas, pineapples, oranges, grapes, figs, strawberries, watermelons, potatoes, tomatoes, cabbage, cauliflower, pease, beans, onions, sweet-potatoes, carrots, beets—all can be and are grown on the island, but in such desultory fashion that the hotel must frequently resort to canned goods or send to Honolulu for supplies.

Of native life there is practically none, and a grass hut is about as much of a novelty here as at Honolulu, where they are modernized to adorn lawns.

Natives and the forest seem dying together.

CHAPTER VII

COMMERCIAL DEVELOPMENT

IT becomes immediately apparent, on study of the subject, (1) that Hawaii has attained its present commercial position entirely through its own resources and the enterprise of its citizens, and (2) that its development has but partially disclosed its natural agricultural wealth. The history of commercial Hawaii may be divided into three eras: (1) sandal-wood, the exportation of which began somewhere about 1800, and had ceased before 1840; (2) whaling, which began in 1819, was at its zenith in 1854, and had disappeared in 1871; and (3) sugar, which first attracted capital (to a very small extent) in 1837, had risen to first importance in 1843, and is to-day the industrial backbone of the islands.

Just when the exportation of sandal-wood began is, I believe, not a matter of authentic record, but, at all events, it gave Hawaiians their first merchantmen vessels, and it plunged the king and his leading chiefs into extravagance and debt.

The sandal-wood gave out long before the debts were paid.

HAWAIIAN-AMERICA

There was no money in circulation until after 1817, therefore all trade was by barter, and great quantities of this precious wood were exchanged for

HAWAIIAN SHARK-TOOTH IMPLEMENTS

ships, to carry still more cargoes of it to China. The rich harvest was a lure irresistible. The chiefs sent their serfs far and deep into the forests; and, indeed, employed them so relentlessly that, it is

COMMERCIAL DEVELOPMENT

said, the serfs deliberately destroyed the young trees, so they might be relieved from toil so heavy in following years.

They judged accurately indeed, for so great was the denudation of the forests that in twenty years sandal ceased to be an important article of export: in twenty more it had practically died out. Two sandal-trees were shown me on the island of Hawaii as rare relics of the great forests which once covered the islands — solitary, almost forgotten, signs of Hawaii's first commercial era.

Though the sandal-trees disappeared, there was left with the king and ruling chiefs the spirit of venture the trade had created—and it had attracted the whalers. The trading spirit sent the coasting-vessels of the king and chiefs on far-off voyages of barter and discovery, and the whalers brought trade, merchandise, and—the missionaries.

It is not my intention to go into details. I purpose merely to show the general disposition of the native and the trend of island trade.

With the decline in sandal-wood trade the whaling interests increased quickly, and so materially as to become the principal business of the islands. The native has never been exacting. Little matters it to him how his stomach is filled, so long as it is filled, and whaling accomplished that end as surely as sandal-wood.

The first white traders at Hawaii were English, who made the islands a point of supply on their trips to the northwest, but they failed to follow up their pioneer advantages, so that the first white traders really to establish themselves were Americans, from New England, who had followed hard on the heels of the whalers from New Bedford and Nantucket. In fact, the traders, whalers, and missionaries fell upon Hawaii simultaneously — the missionaries to accomplish such an evolution in the native from savagery to civilization as has not been equalled in the same length of time elsewhere in the world.

The American whalers made the islands a rendezvous for the majority of all nations fishing in the Pacific, and so close were these interests to those of the islands that laws were made in every way favoring the whalers and their trade, and a wavelet of progression set in motion.

In 1822 printing had been established (though not until 1836 was the first newspaper published, and not until 1843 had one uninterrupted publication), and a year later four American mercantile houses had been opened—two from Boston, one from Bristol, and one from New York. A ship-yard was built in 1825, and Honolulu made a point of transshipment by the whalers, and in 1826 James Hunnewell founded at Honolulu the mercantile house which still exists as C. Brewer & Co. By 1836 interest had deepened and the trade broadened, so that we find salt, Koa lumber, cotton, indigo, corn, potatoes, fruits, hides, Kukui oil, arrowroot, and tobacco on the list of exports.

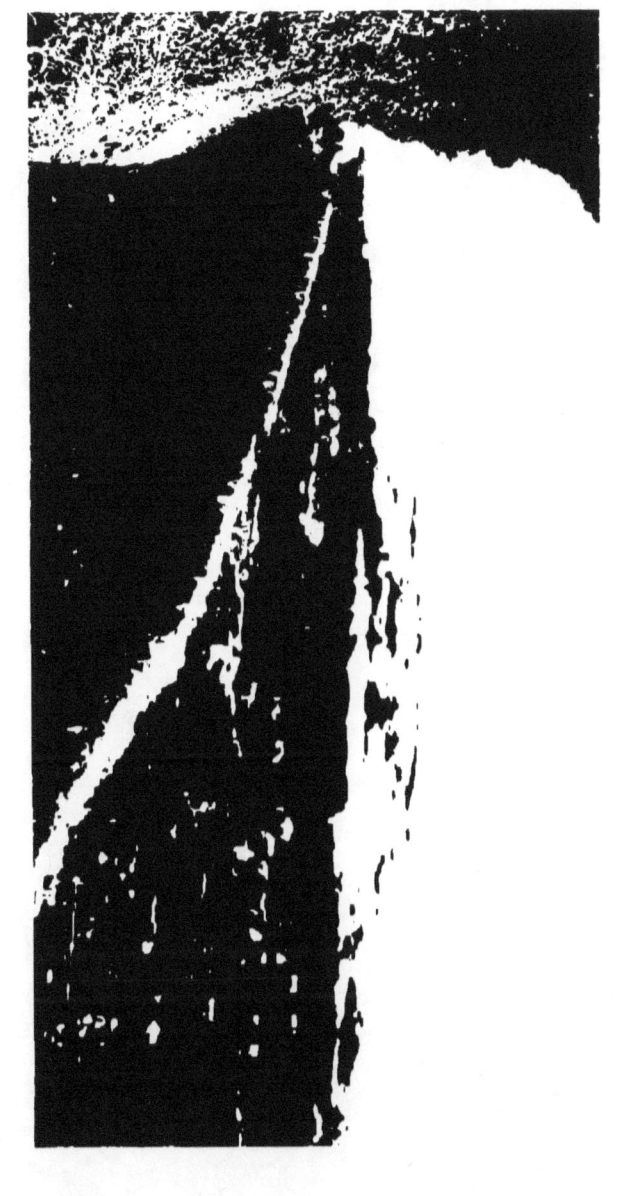

HONOLULU FROM THE PALI   DIAMOND HEAD IN THE DISTANCE

COMMERCIAL DEVELOPMENT

Thus the trade prospered, until, from 1836 to 1841, 447 ships touched at Honolulu, 358 hailing from American (four-fifths whalers) and 82 from English ports, while in the same period Hawaiian commerce showed exports of $338,000 (seeking the far markets of New York, France, and Australia for its produce), and imports of $1,567,000. By 1845 the foreign population of Honolulu was 400, and the shipping owned by residents amounted to $55,000, while the town itself supported five wholesale and twenty retail shops, and one lumber-yard, four hotels, and twelve sailors' boarding-houses and grog-shops. At this time the sugar interests were expanding largely, and some very small and tentative efforts making to plant coffee.

The discovery of gold in California (1848) bore so importantly upon the islands as almost to warrant my classing the nine following years as a separate industrial era in Hawaiian commercial history. Certainly not before had such prosperity come to the islands, although at the beginning of 1849 the outlook was hardly encouraging, for the exodus to California carried away so many of the progressive class that industries on the island came practically to a standstill in 1849, and domestic exports fell from $266,819, in 1848, to $185,083, while imports rose to $729,739.

But 1850 marked the reaction and the increasing trade. The development of the California mining interests created demand for potatoes, meat, flour,

HAWAIIAN AMERICA

and Hawaii found a ready market for all it could raise. This year is a most important one in the commercial development of the Hawaiian Islands, for it marks the first recognition of Hawaii's agri-

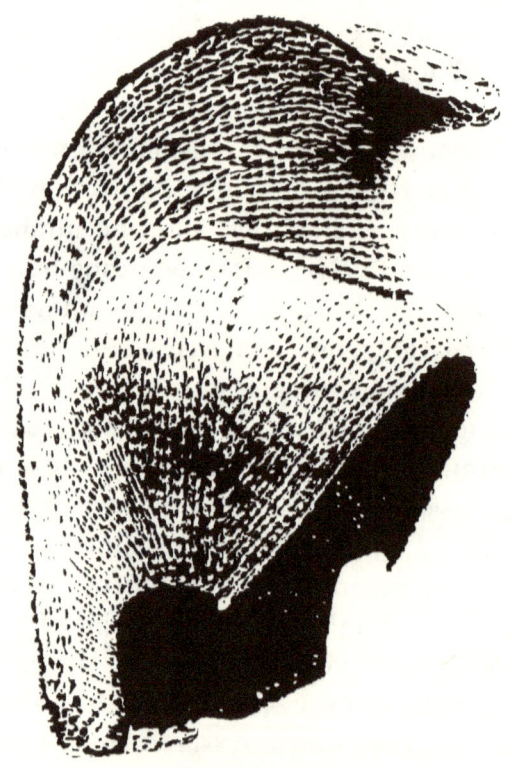

ANCIENT HELMET, WOVEN OF REEDS AND COVERED WITH FEATHERS

cultural possibilities (of which so little general advantage has been taken); organization of an agricultural society: establishment of a postal service;

COMMERCIAL DEVELOPMENT

the visit of 469 merchant-ships (the largest number, in fact, for one year's record), building of a reservoir, and founding of a bank at Honolulu.

It was an active beginning that went busily forward. Wheat was raised, flour-mills erected, and California very largely ate the flour and potatoes of Hawaii's growing until its own heavy-yielding fields overwhelmed all competition.

To-day Hawaii buys all its flour and a heavy percentage of its potatoes in California!

But those were great days for Hawaii—those ten years from 1844 to 1854, which raised the exports from $169,641 to $585,122, the imports from $350,347 to $1,590,837, the custom-house receipts from $14,263 to $152,125, the Hawaiian registered vessels from 15 to 54, the shipping arrivals from 207 in 1844 to 650 in 1854, and with the *Kilauea* brought about (1859) the inauguration of an inter-island steamboat service. This, too, was the heyday of the whale-fisheries, which reached their zenith in 1859, when 549 outfitted in one or another of the Hawaiian ports.

The subsidence, however, of the gold fever on the Pacific coast had a quieting effect on island agricultural business, that decreased materially as California developed its own wealth in that direction. But the set-back was not serious; Hawaiians were beginning to appreciate the richness of their soil, and as its second commercial era was closing— hastened by the destruction (1871) of the whaling fleet in an arctic ice crush—its third was opening auspiciously.

It will enable us the better to appreciate Hawaii's subsequent development if we consider her financial standing at the end of the second era, 1875: Value of imports, $1,505,670, of which $947,260 was from United States; exports, $2,089,736, of

OAHU PRISON (HONOLULU)—FISH-PONDS IN FOREGROUND

which $1,774,083 was for domestic produce; customs receipts, $213,447; Hawaiian registered vessels, 51 of 7136 tons; shipping arrivals (merchantmen), 120 of 93,000 tons; annual taxes, $150,000; population estimated at 57,000; total government revenue (1875), $536,180; public debt, $450,000.

The considerable development of sugar interests in Hawaii was simultaneous with the beginning of an effort, long continued, for closer trade relations with the mainland — as we must call the United

COMMERCIAL DEVELOPMENT

States. So long ago as 1853 it had become apparent that Hawaii, as an outlying sugar plantation of the United States, which in fact precisely describes it, was entitled to recognition as such on the tariff list.

In 1855 a reciprocity treaty was concluded between W. L. Marcy, Secretary of State, acting for the United States, and Judge Lee, Commissioner of the Hawaiian king. Although approved by the Committee on Foreign Affairs, the United States Senate withheld ratification. Again in 1864 the question was raised, but not brought to issue because the public mind was occupied with the Civil War; again in 1867 the treaty was brought forward, ratified by the Hawaiian government, approved by President Johnson and Secretary of State W. H. Seward, but rejected by the Senate.

Yet again, in 1874, the effort to establish closer commercial relations was renewed by King Kalakaua in person visiting the United States with a commission composed of Henry A. P. Carter and Elisha H. Allen, and this time success attended the effort. The treaty (drawn for seven years), signed at Washington, January 30, 1875, and announced by formal proclamation June 3 of the same year, was sufficiently broad in terms practically to create free-trade relations between the United States and the Hawaiian Islands. The United States admitted, free of duty, sugar, and substantially the entire agricultural product of the islands; Hawaii, in turn, opened its ports to the

United States for about every article of domestic consumption on its list.

Protests came at once from Great Britain to the Hawaiian king, and the situation was somewhat strained and uncertain for a couple of years, until the unequivocal and vigorous policy of Secretary of State James G. Blaine settled the matter fairly

HAKALAU LANDING—HOW SHIPS ARE UNLOADED ON THE WINDWARD COAST OF HAWAII

and definitely. In 1884 the treaty was renewed for another seven years, and the exclusive privileges of Pearl Harbor granted the United States, which resulted in further protests, this time from the sugar-refining interests of both Great Britain and the United States. But these also were de-

COMMERCIAL DEVELOPMENT

nied, and the treaty was still in force when annexation came finally in 1898.

With the signing of this reciprocity treaty the Hawaiian industrial and commercial status underwent complete revolution. Though there had always been a healthful amount of enterprise on the islands, the scarcity of labor, the usual failures of crops, and particularly the instability of the degenerating monarchy, filled the way of progression with obstacles, and so beset Hawaii's industrial efforts as to make commercial life one long uncertain struggle. Up to 1876 the financial results of sugar, rice, and coffee growing had not been sufficiently encouraging to warrant or even suggest expansion. It was appreciation of her great possibilities, and realization of her inability to make the most of them under existing trade and political conditions, that incited Hawaii's repeated overtures for reciprocity.

And the significance of reciprocity to the prosperity of the islands now became immediately apparent. Industrial activity was instant and general; thirteen new sugar-plantations were laid out in 1877, fifteen more in the year following; mills were erected, shipping increased, and a general air of hopefulness and confidence spread over Hawaii. How substantial this expansion was may be judged by the importations of 1878 and 1879, which for machinery amounted to $960,342; for hardware and agricultural implements, $414,792; for lumber,

HAWAIIAN-AMERICA

$402,742; and for building materials, $196,554. In 1879 the first railroad on the islands was laid from Kahului (Maui) to Wailuku—for these were the years when the Spreckels sugar interests were developing Maui industries.

It was all outlay in the first two or three years after the ratification of the treaty, but at the end of ten years (1886) the Hawaiian commerce had in-

ANCIENT STONE LAMPS

creased with a great bound, and the annual returns showed: Exports, $10,565,886; imports, $4,877,738; custom-house receipts, $580,444. Shipping arrivals, 310; tonnage, 222,372. Hawaiian registered ships, 58; tonnage, 13,529. Compare these figures with those at the closing of Hawaii's second commercial era in 1875.

COMMERCIAL DEVELOPMENT

The large sugar returns very naturally prompted further expansion, and in 1888 and 1889, responding to the ruling spirit, some of the most extensive plantations on the islands were laid out. Oahu was brought into the line of progression by B. F. Dillingham's enterprise and railroad-building, and by one million and a half dollars' worth of machinery imported by plantations opened as a direct result of the railroad.

Meantime increase in number and considerable improvement in class were making in the several lines of vessels engaging in Hawaiian trade. Not only did the regularly established lines enlarge their facilities, but several new ones were added; and, most important to the islands, a direct semi-monthly service was established between San Francisco and Honolulu. The harbor was dredged and enlarged (1893), a marine railway had been constructed (1883), and Hawaii, from struggling insignificance, had so developed her resources and increased her trade that in 1895 she stood second on San Francisco's foreign-trade list.

At no time during her commercial development, even in the periods of depression, before 1876, had there been panic or failure to meet obligations. No town's business record could be more absolutely unsullied than is that of Honolulu.

And so Hawaii's commerce grew, until at the close of 1896 a cash surplus of $71,000 more in the treasury than at the beginning of the year, after paying all running government expenses and redeeming $16,000 worth of bonds falling due, proved the Republic of Hawaii to be self-supporting, solvent, and prosperous. Perhaps figures will be even more convincing to that end: at the close of 1897, when the last biennial returns were made, Hawaii's imports were $7,682,628; her exports had grown to $16,021,775; custom-house receipts, $708,493. Shipping arrivals 427, tonnage, 513,826. Hawaiian registered vessels 62, tonnage, 34,069. And the Hawaiian balance-sheet on January 1, 1898, showed revenue, $5,042,504; expenditures, $4,654,926; cash balance in treasury, $456,804; value crown and government lands (approximate), $4,500,000; other assets, public buildings, public works, etc., $3,000,000; bonded public debt, $3,679,700.

Rather a tidy showing, considering the length of time and the conditions under which it was made.

CHAPTER VIII

THE LABOR QUESTION

PERHAPS no other feature in Hawaiian industrial life has proved such a boon to those sentimentalists whose habit is to speak twice before thinking once, as the contract-labor system which has ruled on these islands. They have called it Hawaii's "legalized slavery," and likened it unto negro slavery as it formerly existed in the South — comparisons that give fine opportunity for harangue from the rostrum, but in truth reveal the superficiality that appears to be the usual accompaniment of modern sentimentalism. The comparison is absurd, and discloses ignorance, as we shall see.

The general industrial activity following fast upon the signing of the reciprocity treaty in 1875 made it immediately apparent that a very considerable increase of laborers was necessary. The rise of the sugar interests—the development of established plantations, and the laying out of new ones—created a demand for labor which the home or natural market could not supply.

HAWAIIAN-AMERICA

Differing from Cuba or Puerto Rico or the Philippines, which have the advantage of a cheap labor, indigenous and sufficient to supply the needs of many and extensive plantations, Hawaii's native

THE NECESSARY (INDUSTRIAL) EVIL

labor was, and is, neither cheap nor dependable. Therefore it became absolutely necessary to seek help in the labor-markets of the world, and in 1876 a Bureau of Immigration was organized at Honolulu, and vigorous effort put forth to get the labor needed by expanding industry, the hope being held, at the same time, of attracting a class desirable for permanent settlement. With this latter object particularly in view, the bureau sought to encourage immigration of the Portuguese, as an industrious people suited to Hawaiian climatic conditions, and from 1878 to 1887 assisted about 8000 of them into the islands. But their importation proved so expensive that after 1888 no more were assisted until the middle nineties, and Chinese and Japanese, costing greatly less in transportation, were imported instead.

The cost of importing Portuguese was never less than about $240, and sometimes upward of $400, per capita. In one instance a shipment in 1885 cost the government $303, and the planters $115, a total of $418 a man—rather a high premium to pay for labor. The lowest cost to government was $130, and to planter $110, or total of $240 per capita. The cost of getting over the Japanese was $23 to the government, and $64 to the planter, a total of $87 per capita, of which the Japanese returns $60, leaving net cost to government $17, and to planter $10.

In the first ten years of assisted immigration the Hawaiian government expended in round numbers about $1,000,000, and the planters paid out about as much more, the imported labor including (approximately) 9000 Portuguese, 1200 Germans, 200

Norwegians, 900 Polynesians, and 17,000 Chinese (not assisted). No Japanese were imported until 1886, when 1152 men and 252 women arrived, to be so rapidly followed by others that in 1890 there were 12,360; in 1896, 22,329, and at this writing

PORTUGUESE AND JAPANESE WOMEN AS CANE-FIELD LABORERS

there are very probably 30,000 Japanese on the Hawaiian Islands; while the Chinese number about 24,000, and the Portuguese 16,000.

The first shipment of Japanese was gathered from the cities, and proved an undesirable lot, that disregarded agreements and caused the government

THE LABOR QUESTION

and planters much loss of time and money. It was obvious, therefore, some arrangement must be made to guarantee government and planters against loss of the money they advanced to assisted laborers.

Thus began the contract-labor system so disturbing to the sentimentalists!

Let us consider this contract and see how much of "slavery" there is in it. The agreement to which the laborer subscribed was about as follows: (1) That the money for passage from his home to Hawaii be advanced by his employer. (2) That he refund this money at the rate of from one to two dollars a month until it is paid. (3) That he continue with his employer for the full time agreed. (4) That twenty-six days of ten hours each constitute a working month. (5) That he be paid at rates varying from $12 to $15 per month, with free house, firewood, medicine, and medical attendance; in some cases agreements are entered into that provide for the employer furnishing hospital, medicine, attendance, physician, etc., and the laborers contributing each 25 to 50 cents a month towards its support. (6) That he be paid 10 cents an hour for overtime. (7) That his wife, if he has one, be given employment, if she wishes it, at from $7 50 to $10 a month. (8) That he agrees to work faithfully as an agricultural laborer and servant during his term of contract. He need not be separated from his family; he may return to his country or go where he likes at the end of his service.

The contract is voluntarily entered upon and signed by both parties — employer and employé. The employer agrees to find steady work and un-

HOMES OF SUGAR-PLANTATION LABORERS

interrupted pay to the employé for three years. The employé, for his part, agrees to labor on each working-day during that time, except the holidays stipulated in his contract. When his service is concluded, the laborer either remains in the country as an independent worker, or enters upon a new contract, or goes elsewhere. Several thousand Japanese are to-day in the Hawaiian Islands working under their second contract. Sometimes they go home for a little vacation, to enjoy some of the money they have accumulated; more often they continue on the sugar-plantations; just now they are being attracted in large numbers to the coffee industry, by the inducement of a higher wage from the clearing companies, the road-contractors, and the coffee-planters. A considerable percentage of ex-contract laborers plant little patches of cane for themselves on bits of land loaned them by the planters.

The Chinamen from the cane-fields have, as their contracts expired, worked their way into the rice and taro fields, with the result that they have practically absorbed the rice industry of all the islands, and are fast doing as much in taro; the Japanese remaining on the islands as independent workers have drifted more particularly into coffee, and somewhat into small truck-farming for the local market. The Portuguese have practically all remained on the islands at the expiration of the contracts that served to bring them over, and devote themselves to small farming and fruit-growing. In the latter industry they have almost as much of a monopoly as the Chinamen have in rice.

Comparatively few Portuguese, however, are now to be found on the cane-plantations—though their wage runs from $18 to $30 per month, and not a member of the family, old or young, that fails of contributing his or her share of labor. Therefore, as a rule, a Portuguese family saves enough in the first period of their contract to work subsequently for themselves in farming, or in fruit-growing, or in coffee-planting, which is now attracting a great many of them. The industrial and economic ideas of the Portuguese, who want every member of the family at work, clash sometimes with Hawaii's educational laws, which, without distinction as to color, race, or

SUGAR-MILL AND PLANTATION LABORERS' HOUSES

class, insist upon every child between the ages of six and fifteen attending school regularly. On the the whole, however, the Portuguese have proved well worth the original outlay of their importation. They are desirable immigrants, sober and industrious workers, and useful citizens in the development of the islands.

THE LABOR QUESTION

So, too, the Chinese have been and continue a very helpful factor in Hawaii's industrial expansion. They are quiet, industrious, peaceful; occupy a considerable section of Honolulu with their mercantile houses; fill the majority of the trades, and supply the local market with most of its fish and vegetables. Together with the Japanese, they are, too, the domestic servants of the islands. In the canefields they are diligent, obedient, and tractable. Rarely is any trouble had on plantations with the Chinese.

On the other hand, the Japanese is the agitator of the islands. He is the "walking delegate" of Asiatic labor organization; the only Oriental to have been converted to the modern labor union, and, once converted, he has pursued it with the same hysteria that has characterized his adoption of Western ideas generally in Japan. It is only necessary for an idea to come out of the West, and the Japanese seizes upon it with avidity.

The average Japanese day-worker could probably give agitator Debs pointers on the systematic organization of labor. From the Jinrikisha-men through all the various fields of labor up to the skilled trades, the Japanese working-classes at home are powerfully and thoroughly organized and firmly convinced of the efficacy of strikes.

There have been some rather serious times on the sugar-plantations of Hawaii because of these Japanese tendencies, and other times prospectively even more serious have been barely avoided through the interference of the Japanese government. While I was on the islands the Japanese government representative nipped in its incipiency a wholesale strike of Japanese that would for a time nearly have paralyzed the sugar industry. Strikes can perhaps be more disastrous in the sugar industry than in any other; on occasion they might, indeed, cause the loss of the returns of a season's crop. Therefore planters have become rather nervous over the preponderance of Japanese labor in the cane-field, with the leaven of Chinese or Portuguese or others lessening, and a strong desire more nearly to equalize the nationalities is manifest. Chinamen whose contracts have expired are being re-engaged at an increased wage, and an effort is making to recruit 1500 Portuguese from the Azores and Madeira Islands.

The Japanese, who at home earns from $1 30 to $3 90 a month, is a pugnacious, troublesome laborer, vain, slow-witted, impudent, and prone to riot. I was often surprised at the toleration of plantation *lunas* (overseers) in dealing with these surly, cheeky creatures. Not, of course, that all Japanese are so trying, but the average of this kind is sufficiently large to make it formidable, while with the other nationalities trouble is had only in exceptional and individual cases. There are *lunas* who are cruel, sometimes brutal, to the laborers under them, but I am bound to say my investigation in this direction

PLANTING CANE

(and I made an extended one, because of circulated stories of cruelty) disclosed only an occasional brutal *luna*, and he was marked for discipline by the courts and by his employers.

Speaking generally, the care of plantation laborers has been most considerate, and in some instances that came under my observation really paternal. Every district in the islands has its physician, the majority of plantations have hospitals, and one I visited employed nurses at its own expense. I also made it a point to visit the laborers' houses, and in all cases found them sufficient to the needs of the men, and superior to the habitations to which they had been accustomed at home. As these houses are quite similar all over the islands, the illustration presented will give a fair idea of their type and appearance—though not invariably has the occupant the love of flowers and the diligence to beautify the surroundings.

The difference in relationship between the Japanese and the Chinese towards Hawaii is perhaps shown in no way more clearly than by their respective classing on the tax-book. Here we find the Chinese are taxed in real estate to the amount of $1,146,301, the Japanese to the amount of $56,000; on personal property, corporations, mercantile houses, etc., the Chinese are taxed on $2,205,339, the Japanese, $177,307. In Honolulu district alone there are 281 Chinese houses of business, taxed on $446,950, and 55 of Japanese, taxed on $77,700.

The Portuguese, by-the-way, are represented in this district by 18 establishments, taxed on a value of $21,200.

The personal property of the Hawaiians and half-castes is taxed at $1,144,104, or about half the value placed on the property of the Chinese. "Other nationalities," which include Portuguese and small numbers of various foreigners, are taxed on $221,116 personal property, or but very little more than the Japanese. In real estate the Hawaiians and half-castes own $6,958,597, which is just half the combined real-estate holdings of the American, British, and German interests.

There is abundant cause for criticising the labor-contract system of the Hawaiian islands; not, however, that it savored of "slavery"; not that it violated the canons of free labor, or even permitted injustice or cruelty to be visited upon the laborers; not that it failed in any particular to uphold the workman's individual rights. But rather because it surrendered the labor of the islands to the cheap —practically coolie—labor of Asia, and thereby retarded by about twenty-five years at least the prosperous settlement upon the islands of a desirable class.

It will require tireless energy, highest intelligence and management, and a considerable amount of money now to supplant Asiatic with white labor. And yet until that end is accomplished Hawaii will remain undeveloped, much less attain its agricultural possibilities; for no competition is possible between Eastern and Western men in the same field and operating on a common basis. There must be substitution of one by the other.

That the Eastern man gained the ascendency in Hawaii was due to the paucity of the home labor-

PAPAYA TREES

market and to the suddenness and urgency of the demands made upon it. The local labor-market was equal to the country's industrial needs up to the signing of the reciprocity treaty. And then suddenly, with the great boom making in sugar-plantations, there was imperative demand for laborers—thousands of them—which the islands could not supply and America would not send.

No criticism can justly be made on the introduction of Asiatic labor in the early eighties; there was no other recourse. Effort had been made, money spent, to enlist European labor in sufficient quantities, and without success. The sugar industry was developing and required labor, and the Hawaiian planters did what every business man put in the same position would—they got what they could and made the most of it. It is difficult to see what else they could have done in those first days of Hawaii's third commercial era.

The existing labor situation is to be attributed largely to the fact that Hawaii, since 1876, has been overwhelmingly dependent for its commercial existence upon sugar. It is impossible, of course, that the success of an industry which has been the source of the prosperity of all classes in the country, which has been so closely identified with the development of the country indeed, should not be studied diligently and indulgently. Sugar, it must be remembered, has been the very commercial backbone of Hawaii during these twenty-five years of its greatest prosperity.

For the last five years, however, the labor question has been in the hands of the planters, and, I confess, as I rode about the islands it seemed to me they have fallen a long way short of what might

THE LABOR QUESTION

have been accomplished in the way of leavening the Asiatic horde. We can understand the needs of the first dozen years of the sugar industry, and find no fault for the apparent indifference to flooding the country with a class of coolie labor that could never become a part of its permanent prosperity. But for ten years now Hawaiian planters have been amply able to turn from their work long enough to consider the welfare of their country; for just so long at least have they been facing the inevitable and done practically nothing, save to continue seeking cheap Asiatic labor.

We are bound to conclude that greed is the responsible quality for this exhibition.

Hawaii is looking the labor question straight in the face these days: the preponderance of the Japanese and their well-developed tendency to strike and riot, the restriction of Chinese immigration through annexation to the United States, the neglect of industries that should flourish, are suggesting the absolute need to Hawaii's more general prosperity of inducing white labor to enter the country. Many think the budding coffee industry will supply the desired want, and no doubt to an extent it will, but what Hawaii needs is white labor to replace, in large measure, its present coolie labor.

Whence is this labor to come, and what effect will it have on the profits of the sugar industry? These are the questions now before the Honolulu Chamber of Commerce and the Planters' Association, and which they can answer quickly and satisfactorily if the majority are inclined to consider the prosperity of Hawaii above their own swollen dividends.

SETTING OFF FOR THE DAY'S FISHING

There is division of attitude—I cannot believe there is division of opinion—among Hawaiian planters on the labor question. Some are frankly in favor of inducing white-labor immigration, and are indefatigably working to that end; others, and I am bound to say the larger number, profess to see the end of Hawaii's prosperity in the abandonment of coolie labor. They cling to the fallacy that the cheaper the labor the less the cost of production, ignoring entirely the contrary lesson emphasized by their own experience; for to what but intelligent, higher-class, better-paid work, the study of irrigation, of fertilizers, and of machinery, is due the enormously increased production of sugar per acre on Hawaiian plantations?

Manufacturers, planters, traders, the world over, have invariably used that cheap-labor argument in opposing employment of a better class of labor to divert attention from their real motive — disinclination to yield any of their profit. The theory that Hawaiian sugar estates cannot be profitably worked except by coolie labor — as this very low class Asiatic labor must be called — rests wholly on greed. Undoubtedly coolie labor is necessary to the making of dividends that run from thirty to sixty per cent.; but if Hawaii is to increase its population, to develop its other industries — as it must to attain permanent prosperity — a reduction in those sugar dividends is needed. It will be well for Hawaii if more people enjoy the very handsome returns from the sugar industry.

The largest, and therefore the most experienced, employers of labor in the world are united in testifying that the cost of any product is more a question of brain than of cheap labor. The history of America's commerce tends to prove that, as a rule, high wages indicate a low cost of production. How else may be explained the enormous exportation of American high-priced labor goods to low-priced labor countries? How else may be explained the successful competition of the California farmer with India, where the cheapest of cheap labor abounds? Judge Frear, one of Hawaii's stoutest and persistent advocates of white labor, puts the question pointedly to the Hawaiian planters by asking them to "explain the fact that the California farmer pays high wages, high prices for his implements, the expense of transportation by rail to San Francisco, and by seas fifteen thousand miles around Cape Horn to England, the expense of interest, and insurance during this long voyage, and is still able to sell his wheat in the same market and at the same price as the English farmer, who has paid much lower wages, has not had similar expenses of transportation, interest, and insurance, and has obtained his implements at lower prices?"

It is not that white or high-priced labor is prejudiced by Asiatic or cheap labor, in so far as white laborers are paid more; it is not merely because they are white men, or because they want more, or because it costs them more to live, or because, on occasion, there must be recompense for unfamiliar or somewhat trying climatic conditions;

but it is because white or (comparatively) high-priced labor is more capable, has better opportunity, and can earn more. It is cheap in the sense Andrew Carnegie implied when in one of his recent addresses he referred to some of his men as "cheap at $10 per day."

Coolie labor may enable Hawaiian planters to secure for a couple of years longer the extraordinary profits they have realized for several years past, but it will not advance the industry itself, and it will not build up the country. 'Twas not coolie labor that enabled the Hawaiian planters to weather the storm following fast upon the McKinley bill—but the best products of brain, skilfully, diligently employed.

There is literally nothing to support the frequently uttered statement that Hawaiian climate is unsuited to white labor; on the contrary, there is much evidence to confute it. The Portuguese bred in the latitudes of northern California and southern New York have been employed in Hawaii for years, have multiplied and prospered; on Kauai one plantation is manned almost exclusively by Austrians, who are healthful and contented; on Maui, employed in the cane-fields, are a number of Poles, whose reputation for hard, steady work suffers no change in Hawaiian climate; elsewhere in the islands are some 400 Galicians, and all thrive under the new climatic conditions.

White man and negro work in the fields of

Florida, Alabama, and Texas, and the white man does more work, gets more pay, and is less sickly. It is surprising how malignment of Hawaiian cli-

THE TRAVELLER'S PALM

mate with regard to its effect on white labor could so long have been accepted without question. The most trying time of the Hawaiian year is when the

THE LABOR QUESTION

south wind blows; and even then it is not so hot as it is in the wheat-fields of California or in the potato-fields of New Jersey, not to mention Missouri and Indiana or other middle Western states. At all other times of the year Hawaii's fields of labor are delightful, compared with those of the Middle West or the extreme East.

It is not the climate that is faulty in Hawaii: it is those planters who are disinclined to yield any of their immediate profits by offering a wage high enough to attract white-labor immigration. Nor is white labor to be had merely for the asking. All the Western World is asking for laborers. And the United States, instead of having a surplus, is taking them from the Old World at the rate of very nearly three hundred thousand a year! With its many million acres of untilled lands and its wage the highest in the market, the United States is not likely in many years to become naturally an exporter of labor; nor may Hawaii expect to attract the white labor necessary to its upbuilding, unless it offers at least as much as the laborer can get on the mainland. Many reasons may be alleged for shifting labor, but the real reason invariably is search for a larger wage.

While it may not be that Hawaii can attract white labor from America, there remains all of Europe, the world's recruiting-field; and the same energy (with less capital) that characterized the first work of Honolulu's Bureau of Immigration will bring over white labor now just as surely as it brought over the Portuguese in 1878. Immigration from the United States will not come, probably, for several years—not until the odium of coolie labor has been removed; meantime inducements must be offered if white labor from any quarter is to be attracted in appreciable numbers.

One of the few worthy efforts making in this direction at the time of my visit was that by James B. Castle on the co-operative plan. Aside from being a most interesting experiment, it is to be commended for the appreciation it conveys of Hawaii's needs. Mr. Castle's plan includes the payment to each white laborer of $18 a month in addition to furnishing him with house, fuel, a cow, and the exclusive use of ten acres of ground, which the plantation will break up, supply with water for irrigation, transportation for the crop, and buy the cane on the field at the current market-price.

As an acre (on the Ewa plantation, where this co-operative scheme is being tried) will raise, on the average, about sixty tons of cane, and as it takes about seven tons of cane to yield one ton of sugar, at the price current the white laborer would realize about $400 from his ten acres, in addition to his monthly wage, which would bring his total annual income up to $600. Fifty dollars a month, with house-rent, fuel, and cow in addition, is infinitely better wages than the average farm-hand is now getting in the United States, not to mention

THE LABOR QUESTION

Canada or any part of Europe. There is no surer panacea for strikes than a co-operative plan, for under such an arrangement the striking laborer injures himself as seriously as his employer. Last autumn Mr. Castle sent his manager on a recruiting trip to California, and was successful in engaging a number of families that will begin work in Hawaii this spring on this basis.

That this plan can be made a success I have no doubt whatever; that it will be an immediate success I very much question. With the Hawaiian cane-fields monopolized by coolie labor, it will, I think, be some years before the co-operative plan will realize its possibilities — several years, indeed, before any plan short of periodical immigration in large numbers could sufficiently introduce white labor to make an impression on industrial Hawaii.

WOODEN IDOL

It is not that the co-operative plan is lacking in any essential: it is that the Eastern and the Western man cannot be operated on the same basis simultaneously in the same field of endeavor. Whether, in fact, it is or is not a degradation of labor, at least it is thus viewed by white men, and so long as the Japanese and Chinese vastly outnumber all other labor on the sugar-plantations, the result of any scheme introducing a mere handful of white men to labor alongside of the Celestials must be considered as extremely uncertain.

With some fifty-odd thousand Orientals already in residence, there would appear to be enough ' prolong the solution of the labor problem.

Moreover, annexation has checked the flood of Chinese labor Hawaiiwards, seemingly only to open wider the gates for the Japanese.

Whatever may be the action of the Hawaiian planters, there can be no two opinions as to the action needful to Hawaii's future prosperity. White labor is necessary to the further development of the islands, and it must be acquired not in occasional dozens that scarcely are to be discovered in the great mass of coolies, but as it was in the wheat-fields of California and of the middle Northwest, in the potato-diggings of New Jersey and the hop-fields of New York. Individual co-operative plans will undoubtedly accomplish something to this end, but the essential necessity is association by the planters, and a proposition forthcoming to white labor definite enough to be understood, and generous enough to attract in such numbers as may speedily leaven the Japanese-Chinese elements.

CHAPTER IX

INDUSTRIAL PROSPECTS

THERE are three serious hinderances to the industrial development of Hawaii: (1) large individual holdings of land; (2) contract labor; (3) exorbitant transportation rates—inter-island as well as between the group and the mainland.

Until one has studied the situation deeply, one wonders how it is that Hawaii, with a climate unexcelled, and a soil capable of producing the majority of both temperate and tropical products, nevertheless imports the bulk of its food. Although in the fifties, and a bit later, Hawaii supplied the Pacific coast with wheat and potatoes, it now spends abroad over one million dollars annually for food deficits of man and beast, the greater proportion of which could be and should be raised on the islands. Of this amount nearly $300,000 goes for hay and grain, and $80,000 for dried fish, although the waters surrounding the islands teem with fish!

But perhaps the most surprising importation is

HAWAIIAN-AMERICA

that of fresh fruits, to the amount of $17,000, although the possibilities of Hawaii's fruit yield, if properly developed, are limited only by the needs of a continent. Never is there frost in the islands below an altitude of 5000 feet, so practically all

PINEAPPLE RANCH, BEFORE FRUITING

tropical fruits are possible, even the papaya, the pomelo, the alligator-pear. There is no limit to the banana possibilities—the banana, which, with dishevelled top, is found even wild (though non-productive in that state) all over the islands—and yet the annual export ($75,000) does not equal the

INDUSTRIAL PROSPECTS

importation of dried fish. Pineapples could be raised in sufficient quantities to supply the United States, yet the actual export ($14,000) is several thousand dollars less than the fruit imports from California. And these two products stand respectively fifth and seventh on Hawaii's export list, and neither industry is progressing prosperously. Indeed, the banana industry has rather declined, the 1897 export being $50,000 behind that of 1896, and $25,000 less than the smallest year since 1893.

All industrial thought in Hawaii is for sugar and rice and coffee. Island residents have been sugar-mad for a dozen years, and are rapidly becoming demented over coffee. Meantime all the other industries—existent and possible—languish or are entirely neglected, and the unique economic and social relations on the islands rather tend to nourish such a condition.

All Hawaii is practically divided into great baronial estates, so to say, with a few lords of the land, their time-servers (the contract laborers), and a comparative handful of independent laborers, who are wage-earners only, and no factor whatever in the development of the country.

For instance, practically all the land on the island of Kauai is either owned outright or held on long lease by six men. Even if a native or other resident had a few hundred dollars and wished to invest in a small farm on that island or other local agricultural industry, he could not do so; he could not purchase the land. I met a man in Kauai who for several years unsuccessfully endeavored to buy from its owner just enough land in the little settlement where he lived upon which to erect his shop, but was compelled finally to build on leased ground.

A few of these large landholdings are owned outright—as, for instance, the Bishop estate, which includes nearly 600,000 acres, and is scattered over several islands of the group—but most of them are held on long lease from the government. The majority of these leases were given in 1883, and their average life is thirty years, though those on Oahu are mostly for forty years, and many of them have the privilege proviso of renewing for periods of equal length.

Thus the agricultural expansion, if any there is to be, must be brought about through the reclaiming of government land, now mostly unsurveyed and overrun with jungle. And, to be even more explicit, I may add that the island of Hawaii is the only one offering material possibilities in this direction. Whatever land there is on Oahu, Maui, or Kauai—not already owned or under long lease—may be put down at once as unworthy of consideration. In Hawaii, however, the government has been making every effort within its means to open the country for settlement, though as yet the demand is only for coffee-land, and the small farmer has not begun to arrive.

PINEAPPLE FIELD, IN FRUIT

INDUSTRIAL PROSPECTS

Meantime the Agricultural Bureau of the government is making intelligent effort to further what there are of the small farming interests. In the sale of all lands nowadays a forest reservation to conserve moisture is required, with the idea of checking the fast-dying forests of the islands. Foresters and gardeners are employed planting and caring for young trees, and every year a considerable number are used in the reclothing of the denuded country. Money is lacking for a suitable experimenting station, but a nursery has been finally established at Honolulu, and seeds are imported and tried, and, by way of encouragement, sent to the farmers.

Intelligent direction and effort are required, and some energy; and there is needed, too, material encouragement to attract small-farmer immigration.

In Honolulu—and there is not another settlement save Hilo, on the island of Hawaii, that has any urban pretensions—are shops and mercantile houses usual to towns, and having no proprietary connection with the plantations. But there is no class that on its own account is developing the country—none between the great estate-holders and the hireling tillers of the soil. This is why the natural agricultural advantages of Hawaii have been neglected. The "barons" turned to sugar as the most profitable product, and the others, though always earning a good wage, had neither land to cultivate nor capital to invest.

The physical characteristics of the islands are similar. Each is divided by a ridge, or backbone, of mountains, with climate and products on one side differing somewhat from those on the other. The windward side is usually cooler, though more tropical, because moister. Especially is this true of the island of Hawaii—very considerably the largest of the group—where the contrast of the windward with the leeward side is as that of perpetual spring with dry and dusty summer. The forests are broken by chasms, and now and again you come to deep conical pits that in times past have been active craters.

The coast-lines are very irregular, particularly those to the windward, which are ragged and picturesque. Therefore harbors are lacking, though there are numerous channels in reefs affording entrance into basins.

Honolulu has really the only completed harbor of the islands where steamers land at a pier; elsewhere the small inter-island steamers lie out in an open road, and freight and passengers are taken off in small boats, sometimes through the surf, on to the beach—more frequently at a small landing.

Speaking generally of the islands, the soil yields very little spontaneously, but under irrigation seems capable of producing heavily, and almost anything fitting that is planted. The quality of the soil, however, varies considerably. There are great stretches of land that seem unsuited for any

INDUSTRIAL PROSPECTS

purpose save pasturage, and other great stretches apparently not even so desirable. In other places

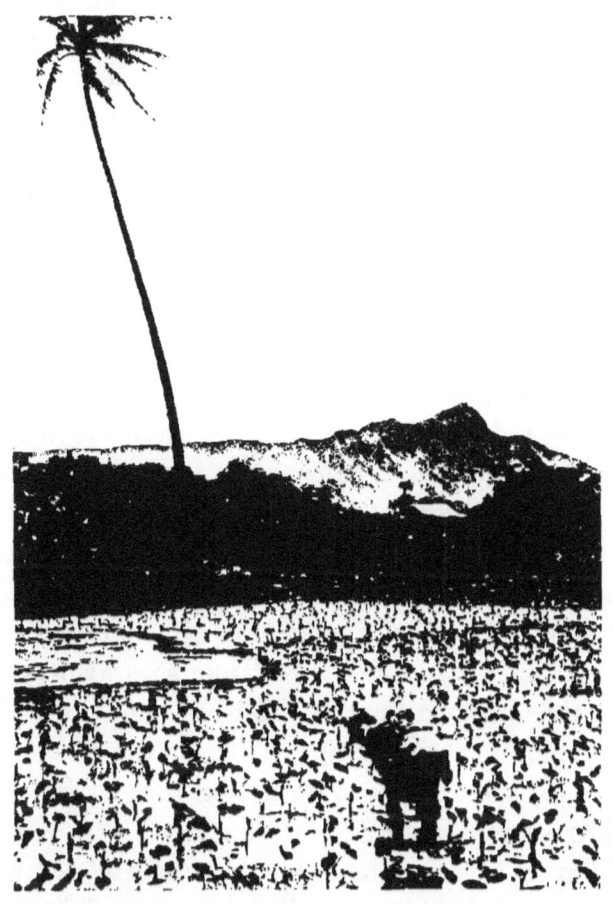

LOWLAND TARO CULTIVATION

again the soil is formed of decomposed volcanic matter, sand, mud, and ashes, and is very fertile.

But the richest land of the islands is in the valleys, which for ages have been receiving the débris and rains of the mountains, the accumulated deposits of vegetable mould, and are exceedingly rich and productive. The number of these valleys is limited, however, and are entirely given over to the rice and taro industries.

Rice is for export, and taro is the bread and meat of the native. Both industries are now almost entirely in the hands of the Chinese, whereas taro formerly was as exclusively cultivated by the native. The rice-fields, with their little white fluttering flags planted at frequent intervals over the ripening crop, and the tiny yet noisy wooden windmills to scare off robber birds, everywhere mark the valley landscape; while the rice-threshing floors, rolled out hard and clean and smooth—light-colored squares in the deep-green surrounding—are to be seen in every fair-sized patch of rice cultivation. Now and again one sees also even a primitive mill to supply local consumption. The Chinamen get two crops in the year from their fields, for which they pay annual rent of from $25 to $30 an acre, including water.

Taro is a cross between a yam and a sweet-potato, and one square mile, so it is said, will produce enough to feed 15,000 natives. Certainly no one who has eaten taro would question the statement, for it is very substantial, and the superabundance of adipose tissue with which the average

INDUSTRIAL PROSPECTS

native is burdened surely suggests its nourishing properties. There is upland and lowland taro, the former growing dry, and the latter in water, like rice, and it may be cooked in various ways, like the potato, though the native takes it most frequently baked, and as *poi*.

Poi is the national dish of Hawaii, and has the great advantage of being cheap and fattening—formerly the native took as much pride in his particular brew of *poi* as some good housewives do in their biscuits, but now, alas! his pride has departed, and this industry too has fallen into the hands of ever-watchful John Chinaman.

And the making of *poi* is no easy task—perhaps that explains the natives' retirement from the work. Taro is a tough, fleshy root, and in the first *poi*-making stage it must be ground to a flour. This could, of course, be done by machinery, but that would not be Hawaiian; therefore, as in the old days, the tough root is brought to the desired condition by a stone pestle and a wooden—sometimes stone—trough. After its reduction to flour it is then worked into a thinnish paste, and if the best article of *poi* is desired, it is permitted to ferment before being served in the calabash, as the wooden bowl—the only native dish—is called.

Usually one calabash answers for a family, which, squatting around the common bowl, feeds by skilfully gathering a quantity of *poi* on the fingers, and then with equal dexterity transferring the mess to the mouth. According to its consistency, it may be "one-finger," "two-finger," or "three-finger" *poi*, the index-finger being equal to the task of the

CARVED LADLE

feeding if the *poi* is quite thick, and three fingers required when at its thinnest. It is an acquired taste to the foreigner, but many of them appear to acquire it readily enough: the white Hawaiians take their *poi* and *squid* (as the dried tentacles of the octopus are called) with apparently as much relish as the native. It was tasteless to my palate, unless perhaps it suggested starch. The modern-made *poi*, unless you get into the house of an old native who has not lost pride in the art, is lavender in color, but the real article is pink —the color formerly demanded of all *poi* served to royalty.

Something might be accomplished towards supplying at least the home market with vegetables and fruit were the inter-island freight rates not so high as to be almost prohibitive, and certainly very discouraging. To ship cattle weighing from 300 to 400 pounds from Hawaii to Oahu (150 to 190 miles) costs $4 50 per head; it is 70 miles to Maui from Honolulu, and 2100 from San Francisco to Honolulu, yet California supplies the Hon-

INDUSTRIAL PROSPECTS

olulu market with the bulk of its potatoes, notwithstanding California raises two crops a year,

BREAD-FRUIT TREE

while in Hawaii they ripen the year round; butter also comes from the Pacific coast, since island butter is 50 cents a pound, while the California article can be sold at Honolulu for 45 cents. Considering the farming opportunities on every hand, the Hawaiian prices are extravagant. Eggs, for instance, are 45 cents a dozen—sometimes 60 cents, sometimes so low as 30 cents; flour is $1 50 per sack of 50 pounds; oranges, 25 cents a dozen; grapes, 15 cents a pound; strawberries, 20 cents a pound. In grain the prices are still higher—oats are $2\frac{1}{4}$ cents per pound, and corn 2 cents. Lumber is $20 per 1000 square feet.

With its present population of great landholders, natives (of small means, if not impecunious), and contract laborers, little, if anything, can be expected in the way of general industrial development, and that little just now is making in the direction of coffee, the only apparent opening for the settler of smaller means. There is land enough of a kind to be had, but there are none of the small-farmer type of settler already in the islands with sufficient means and energy to utilize it, and the land of itself is not sufficiently valuable to attract that class of immigrant from abroad.

Until some effort succeeds in setting such a wave of immigration towards the islands, Hawaii will continue, as it is now, the most expensive of civilized countries in which to live.

Quite a number of natives and half-castes and others, acting under the special homestead provision in the Land Act of 1895, took up small holdings, which, in the majority of cases, have finally passed out of the possession of the original settlers. But these, in almost every instance, are merely homes, with perhaps a garden only large enough to supply the needs of the family. They take no part in an industrial movement. What native fruit and vegetables do find their way to the markets are grown by the Portuguese and the Chinamen, who rent small fertile patches that are to be spared from the rice-fields in the valleys, or are to be found on the edges of Honolulu.

The land held in large holdings is either devoted to sugar or to cattle, or, if suited to neither of these industries, it lies fallow. There is quite a number of cattle, especially on the island of Hawaii, but the industry is not followed to its limit. The ranges are covered with a short, only fairly nutritious (hilo) grass, but the cattle seem to keep in very fair condition, though the high grades do not thrive in low latitudes, and the native stock is never so large nor the best beef. Hawaii could greatly increase both the quality and quantity of its cattle-raising by pursuing the industry more intelligently and less extravagantly. Corn is necessary to put the stock on the market in prime condition; but although there is scarcely a cattle-range where corn would not flourish at a very small outlay of either time or money, the cattle-men get their corn from California and pay two cents a pound for it!

Even as it is, the local markets are all supplied with native beef, and hides are fourth on the list of exports, and increasing.

Sheep-raising is pursued vigorously, but confined to a couple of islands, largely waterless and unsuited to other industries, and to a few individuals with large investments. It is decidedly a limited

UPLAND TARO

industry, though it can hardly be said to be falling behind, the export of wool remaining sixth on the Hawaiian list.

Both cattle and sheep were, by-the-way, introduced to the Hawaiian Islands by Vancouver in 1793-'4, and for the first ten years were declared *tabu*.

With the exception of such varieties as may require frost to give them the desired flavor, all the

INDUSTRIAL PROSPECTS

fruits and vegetables of the temperate, and most of those of the tropic, zones have at times flourished in the Hawaiian Islands. Under intelligent cultivation and with needed irrigation (in some sections), the soil apparently has no limit in productiveness. And although practically all the fruits, and certainly all the vegetables, of Hawaii were originally imported, yet they thrive equally as well as at home.

Tobacco of an excellent quality has been produced, tea grown, hemp (sisal) raised and found of satisfactory fibre, and even cotton produced. Indeed, cotton from 1863 to 1866 became quite an item, in a small way, of Hawaiian commerce. In 1866, 22,289 pounds were exported, but the industry declined with the resumption of activity in the Southern States of the United States, and ceased in 1874. With new markets opening in Japan and China, Hawaii as a cotton-producer contains possibilities worth looking into.

There are few destructive insects in Hawaii, but those few are industrious and deadly. There is the Japanese beetle, which has killed all the roses; a species of caterpillar, which eats grass to its very roots, and voracious worms in all newly turned fields. But Hawaii is well prepared to fight the insect pests by having in government employ Professor Albert Koebele, an entomologist of marked ability, whom California was short-sighted enough to let slip because of a penny-wise, pound-foolish policy rampant in its Agricultural Bureau. There is, however, another pest—lantana—not an insect, that, while not so insidious, is perhaps as bothersome. Lantana, like most of Hawaii's ills, is of foreign origin. It is a low, vine-like bush of utmost toughness that, once having gained a hold, sweeps over the country like wild-fire. Several planters told me that keeping lantana under control was one of their considerable items of expense.

Now as to climate. A great deal is said by certain white residents in favor of the Hawaiian climate when the islands are under discussion as a resort for tourists and other pleasure or health seekers; and a great deal is said by the same gentlemen to its discredit when discussed as a field for white, and especially for American, labor.

In point of fact, the climate of Hawaii is perhaps not excelled anywhere else on earth. Large enough as the islands are to have a character of their own, and still in no way to neutralize the peculiarly desirable quality of oceanic environment, the Hawaiian climate is midway between temperate and tropical; tender, yet not enervating; breezy, though not boisterous; with sunshine from which you need no protection, and a rainfall that does not become monotonous.

A veritable land of sunshine and breezes, whose temperature you may vary as you choose from sea-level up to Mauna Kea (13,825 feet). You may leave one side of an island in a rain-storm, and find

INDUSTRIAL PROSPECTS

sunshine on the other; but though there is considerable variety in this respect, the temperature is about uniform, and at sea-level is 74° Fahrenheit. Taken by the year, this average does not vary over a degree one way or the other; taken by the month, the average of the coldest month is 69°, and of the warmest 78°. The extreme lowest temperature is 50°, the highest 90°; and either of these figures has been reached only once in the last dozen years. The average daily range at Honolulu is 11°, and its usual temperature is several degrees cooler than the average of a number of other cities in the same latitude—notably Havana.

The northeast trade-winds are the saving feature of the Hawaiian Islands, imparting uniform temperature, healthfulness, and tonicity. The record for fifteen years shows that the least number of trade-wind days per year was 225—the greatest 301—the mean 258. January has a normal average of 14 days of trades, which, as the sun moves north, increase until the normal average reaches $29\frac{1}{2}$ days in July and August, and then begins a corresponding diminution through the autumn months to the end of the year.

Oahu and Kauai, of the group, are mostly influenced by these trade-winds, which may there be said to blow for nine months of the year. Maui, which is larger, has a few places to leeward, like the town of Lahaina, for instance, where there is a regular land and sea breeze; and Hawaii has a land and sea breeze all the year round. The winter is the least desirable part of the Hawaiian year, for at that time the northeast trade-winds are interrupted, and winds from the south and west often

MAKING POI—POUNDING THE TARO

prevail for weeks. The south wind, which the natives aptly call the "sick-wind," brings rain and often ailment to susceptible foreigners; but there are never hurricanes, and only rarely thunder-storms.

INDUSTRIAL PROSPECTS

This is the time, too, of the "Kona storms" (*makani Kona*), which come out of the south and west, and sometimes for a week hold a section in the gloom of rain and wind before they finally wear off to the northwest and the country smiles again. The most delightful months of the year are April, May, June, July, and September. The yearly average rainfall of Oahu is about 40 inches; of Maui, 25 to 30; of Kauai, 55; and on Hawaii, with its dry side and its very wet side, it varies so much as to necessitate more detailed figures; in the Kona coffee belt, on the dry side, the average rainfall is about 60 inches; in the Olaa district it is 175 inches; in the Hilo forest, 200 inches; and immediately around the town of Hilo, from 130 to 150 inches.

What particularly impressed me in the Hawaiian climate—and I cite my experience because I do not, as a rule, care for these too balmy climes—was the absence of an enervating quality. Some say that such an influence does attend upon long residence on the islands, but my investigations suggest that only white women who never take exercise are so affected. The Hawaiian-born children of foreign parents bloom like the foliage under which they play; it would be difficult indeed to improve on the physique of the boys and young men born of white parents in Hawaii, whom I saw swimming, yachting, rowing, and on the streets of Honolulu. Those in the United States who really wish to see what Hawaiian climate does for children of white parentage should view the members of the "Hawaiian Club" at Yale or at Harvard. It is a notable fact that the white-born Hawaiians who have come to American universities have been above the average in physical attainments, as the athletic records attest; and I have in mind

PULULA-TREE, FROM LEAVES OF WHICH THE NATIVE HUT IS MADE

four sons (of one distinguished family) at Yale, whose physical magnificence would boom any climate or stir pride in any mother's heart, wherever it beat.

Men and women who take no exercise find semi-tropical climates enervating in time. It is the law of the human system and of the land.

INDUSTRIAL PROSPECTS

The tropics, of course, are really trying, and perhaps one of the most surprising sights to the newly arrived at Singapore is Englishmen playing cricket in the heat of the day on the Esplanade. But the cricket, and the golf, and the riding, and the polo, and the walking, and (in some sections) the football are just what keep the Far Eastern Englishman fit.

If men or women wish to keep healthful in the tropics, they must take some exercise; it is imperative. In the semi-tropics it is helpful.

It is natural to conclude this chapter with a word or so on the islands as a field of venture for the individual immigrant.

Let me say at the outset that Hawaii is no land of promise for indigent adventurers; neither is there here an agricultural bonanza. The islands can easily support a very much greater number of people than now live upon them, but it will not be until there has been a decided readjustment of the land, labor, and transportation questions.

The great industry is the production of sugar, which requires large capital. The rice industry is in the hands of the Chinese, and there is no public sugar or rice land to be had. The coffee industry is really the only one offering immediate opportunities to the immigrant, but for the development of a coffee-plantation of even moderate size some capital is needed; land cannot be had now for perhaps less than $50 an acre, and it would take $30 per acre more to clear it, not to mention the knowledge required, or the cultivation of the trees for five years, until some adequate return is had.

There are opportunities in fruit-growing—if the steamer rates are ever lowered—and in fruit-canning; but these also require capital. There is a field of endeavor in raising grapes, oranges, lemons,

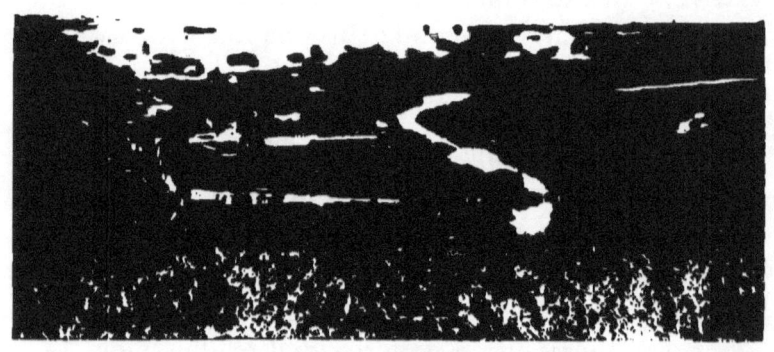

ONE OF THE RICE-GROWING VALLEYS

vegetables, which now come from California, because no one supplies the Hawaiian market; but all these demand small capital. Not only capital, but brains and industry and skill.

The government is surveying as rapidly as possible land that is to be thrown open to settlement, but it is put on the market slowly, and never in quantities sufficient for any considerable number of new-comers.

INDUSTRIAL PROSPECTS

The new lands on the island of Hawaii are off the (at present) one road, although other roads are soon to be constructed. The low-lying flat lands with abundant water-supply are all taken up. There does remain a considerable area to be disposed of as surveys are completed and as old leases expire, principally lands suited to coffee cultivation. Small farming, as I have said, is greatly handicapped by the high inter-island transportation rates.

With this data in hand, gathered by my personal tour of the islands, the best advice I can give to those looking Hawaiiwards is to reiterate that offered by Mr. J. F. Brown, the public-lands agent:

Don't go to Hawaii as a sort of forlorn hope, without experience, without money — trusting to good-luck.

Don't go to plant coffee without necessary capital.

Don't expect to find a country where hard work, care, and economy are not necessary.

Don't go without getting trustworthy information in advance.

But if you do go, after finally considering the matter, and take experience and energy and sufficient capital to insure you against want, and to enable you to study the situation on the ground before making a final decision, you will be warmly welcomed; and what has been a kindly country to others may also prove so to you.

CHAPTER X

SUGAR-GROWING

THE development of the sugar industry is so closely identified with the development of Hawaiian commerce as to make separate discussions almost supererogatory. Sugar is practically Hawaii's commerce, and Hawaii's commerce is substantially sugar. Of the 1897 export figures of $16,021,775, sugar represented $15,390,442 (and of this total, $15,390,223 came to the United States). Incidentally let me note that of the thirty millions of dollars invested in Hawaiian sugar-plantations, twenty-two and one-half millions are American; of the total population of the island (109,020), nearly one-quarter (24,653) are employed on the sugar-plantations; of the Chinese and Japanese inhabitants (45,000), almost half (21,000) are employed on the sugar-plantations. With this array of figures confronting him, the doubting reader will hardly challenge my statement of sugar's relation to Hawaiian commerce.

Sugar-cane is one of the comparatively few indigenous products of the Hawaiian Islands — for,

SUGAR-GROWING

strange to relate, with the exception of a few varieties, all the trees, flowers, and fruits that now flourish were introduced by the early white settlers; not even the banana is indigenous; and the present cocoa-palms that picturesquely fringe the Hono-

AN OAHU SUGAR-PLANTATION PUMPING-STATION

lulu harbor were all planted — every one of them. However, as sugar-cane is mentioned by Captain Cook in 1778 — before there were any whites on the islands — we may accept it as having been native to the soil. We know there are abundant statements from old natives that it grew wild and luxuriantly in the valleys and on the lowlands, but no use was made of it except in its raw state for food.

One of the earliest of Hawaiian planters, L. L. Torbert, claims to have traced the first sugar-manufacturing to a Chinaman, who in 1802 arrived at Honolulu on one of the vessels trading in sandalwood, with a stone mill and boilers, and ground off one small crop, which he made into sugar before returning home with his apparatus. We must take Mr. Torbert's unsupported word for this, for the earliest otherwise authenticated record of sugar-making is that of a Don Paulo Marin, who had the cane mashed on large wooden platters (*poi* boards) by the natives with their stone *poi* pounders, and then collecting the juice, boiled it in a small copper kettle. Mr. H. P Baldwin, one of the oldest and most experienced planters on the islands, vouches for this. It is a matter of little moment, I suppose, who made the first sugar, though there is some satisfaction in collecting these details for this chapter.

At all events, various accounts agree as to the manufacture of sugar and molasses in several quarters at about the year 1823, and it is undoubted that the first mill of any consequence was erected at Koloa (Kauai) by Dr. R. W Wood in 1835. This first mill, and all others for fifteen years, were crude in form and wasteful in process; a native grass house commonly answered as mill, the rollers were wooden, and the kettles whalers' try-pots, while the

HARVESTING THE SUGAR-CANE

motive power was furnished by oxen, horses, or in some cases by water. The sugar, of course, was of a single grade, and that inferior, it was the residue after the juice had been boiled to a thick syrup and drained off through the perforated bottoms of barrels.

Nevertheless, there was some exporting of sugar, a surprising amount considering the slow and primitive process: in 1837 $300 worth was exported, and this was increased to $6200 in 1838, and to $18,000 in 1840. Mr. Baldwin tells of a mill he remembers, between 1840 and 1850, which "consisted of three whale-ship try-pots set on adobe and stone mason-work, the rollers being wooden, strengthened with iron bands"; I am told, too, that the first centrifugal machine used in any country for drying sugar was invented by D. M. Weston, a resident of Hawaii, and used on a Maui plantation in 1851.

But the sugar-market was restricted and fickle, and the industry at this period had so many discouragements it finally began to lose ground, so that by 1857 the plantations had diminished to five. A decided change for the better, however, came with the adoption of steam as the motive power in 1858-9, and two years later, when the first of the modern vacuum-pans were introduced, the number of plantations rose to twenty-two, of which nine ground by steam and twelve by water. Like the commerce of the islands, the sugar industry has thrived in eras, each fostered by some new impetus, each more successful than its immediate predecessor.

The first real impetus to cane-growing came with the outbreaking of the American Civil War and the consequent inflation of sugar values; the second was given by the reciprocity treaty with the United States in 1876, and the third has been furnished within very recent years by irrigation.

How these eras have affected the output is best told by the figures: in 1863 about 2600 tons were exported; in 1876, upwards of 13,000 tons; and in 1896, 240,000 tons; and it is not at all unlikely that this year (1899) the figures will reach 260,000 tons. It is interesting to note further, while we are on comparative figures, that the exports of sugar compared with the labor employed in its cultivation and manufacture, during the last three years estimates have been made, show the following gradual increase: "1895, nearly $7\frac{1}{3}$ tons per capita employed; 1896, a little over $9\frac{1}{3}$ tons; and in 1897, very nearly $10\frac{1}{2}$ tons."

There are sixty plantations on the islands, of which fifty own mills and have all needed machinery for the manufacture of sugar. Practically all of these use the crushing process—which the most experienced planters on the islands prefer. The diffusion process was introduced about 1887, the first plant being erected at Kealia (Kauai), others following, until there were half a dozen; but the improvement in the crushing process has arrested

HAULING CANE TO THE MILL.

the attention diffusion methods were diverting. The diffusion process saves within five per cent. of the sugar in the cane, whereas the mills lose from ten to eighteen per cent. On the other hand, the diffusion plant necessitates the extra cost of fuel, whereas in the mill the cane pulp — or bagasse, as the cane is called when the juice has been crushed from it — supplies all the fuel necessary. Moreover, the constant increase in number of rollers in the mills is steadily lowering the percentage of sugar lost in the crushing process, and experts are confident that before improvement ceases the average extraction in the mills will very nearly equal that by the diffusion plant. As it is, there are very few diffusion plants, and planters claim that the cost of manufacture is less and the general results more satisfactory by the crushing process.

Nowhere else is there equal cultivation of the soil or such care of the cane as in Hawaii. Laboratories in many instances are connected with the mills; the soil is analyzed before the planting, and fertilized according to its need; steam-ploughs are used where the conformation of the land will permit of it; the mills are the best money can buy, and as competition in the manufacture of machinery is sharp, almost every year adds some new and scientific improvement. I may add, by-the-way, that the McKinley bill repealing the duty on sugar was somewhat of a blessing in disguise to these islands, although it was at the time a heavy blow (the price of sugar falling from $100 to $60 per ton in one day), as under the treaty Hawaiian sugar entered the United States duty free. But meeting the prices and output of other sugar-producing countries necessitated abandonment of the simpler methods that were profitable enough with high prices and no competition, and started the movement which resulted in Hawaii having the finest machinery in existence—substantially all American made. Last year the nine-roller Ewa mill on Oahu turned out 140 tons of sugar each running day.

The islands of Hawaii are all very much alike in conformation; each has its backbone of mountain, with land more or less broken by ridges and gulches, reaching to the sea; in some of the islands deep valleys escape from the centre, where the mountains have been rent by volcanic action into abrupt chasms, and run to the very water's edge. The soil of the valleys is very rich indeed, and invariably planted in rice; the sugar lands are those along the coast of the islands, extending back to an elevation of about fifteen hundred feet, beyond which is coffee land or pasture. And wherever there is land fit for growing sugar, there cane will be found, either planted or immediately prospective. There is practically now no land on the Hawaiian Islands capable of raising cane profitably that is not so employed.

Improved machinery and fertilization have tremendously increased the annual sugar yield, but

CANE PILED ALONG RAILROAD, READY FOR TRANSPORTATION TO MILL.

the real developer of Hawaiian plantations in recent years has been irrigation, which has reclaimed for cane much land previously considered irredeemable. Practically all plantations on Oahu, Kauai, and Maui irrigate their cane; the rainfall of windward Hawaii, where are the majority of the plantations, is quite heavy, while on the leeward side, in the section where cane is planted, the land is sufficiently near the mountains to insure a dependable rainfall. Yet in some parts of leeward Hawaii water is run from the mountains down upon the lowland cane-fields. On Kauai water is taken by some of the plantations from the mountains that occupy the centre of the island; but the usual system of irrigation throughout the islands is by means of wells, a pumping plant, and a reservoir system.

On no island is this plan carried out so elaborately or with such handsome results as on Oahu, where the natural richness of the soil has been increased twofold. Pumps are now used which have a capacity of ten million gallons in twenty-three hours, and it is intended to employ one with a capacity of twelve million gallons. At present water is being pumped to an elevation of 350 feet, but a plant was being put in while I was in Oahu sufficiently powerful to raise water 525 feet, and some of the most progressive of the planters expect to finally irrigate cane 650 feet above the water-source. Thus far, despite the great number of wells that have been sunk on the same plantation and on plantations contiguous, no diminution in the water-supply is apparent.

The average yield of sugar to the acre of cane is greater in the Hawaiian Islands than in any other cane-growing country in the world. It varies, however, a great deal; the average yield of Maui, for instance, is about three and one-half tons of sugar to the acre; Hawaii's average is lowered by the smaller producing qualities of her leeward or dry side, but would not go lower than four tons; Kauai, from four to five tons; and Oahu, six to seven tons. There are, of course, pieces of ground, even entire plantations, on every one of these islands, where the yield would greatly exceed the average of the island; one plantation on Oahu, for instance, yields ten tons of sugar to the acre (it takes seven to eight tons of cane to produce a ton of sugar), and special yields of even sixteen tons per acre have been obtained from given sections of the same Oahu plantation. The quality of these figures is the better appreciated by comparison with the yields of Louisiana and Cuba.

The average yield of Louisiana—according to the figures Professor W. C. Stubbs, Director of the State Experiment Station, has been kind enough to furnish me—varies from one ton to two and one-half tons of sugar per acre, the average being perhaps not over one and one-half tons. This is not the yield of the best sugar-houses individually, but

THE RESULT OF AN EXPANDING COMMERCE—CANE HAULED TO MILLS BY STEAM-POWER

SUGAR-GROWING

it is the average of the aggregate production of the State. While there are in Louisiana a considerable number of sugar-houses with the very latest improved machinery and mills, extracting as high as eighty per cent. of the weight of the cane, still there are remaining a few old-fashioned open-kettle sugar-houses that do not extract more than fifty or sixty per cent. of the juice, and cannot remove more than one hundred pounds of sugar per ton of cane. Happily for the future of this industry in Louisiana, these are disappearing very rapidly, and in their place the improved sugar-house is being erected and developed.

Cuba's cane-raising possibilities have never been fully realized. The yield per acre prior to the war was very light, because of the general agricultural deficiency of the island, due to Spanish corruption, Cuban lack of enterprise, and the troublous times; certainly not to any deficiency in the soil, as the fact that they carry the cane to the sixth and even to the twelfth ratooning indicates. Ratooning means cutting the cane at the ground's edge and leaving the root to sprout the next year—so a sixth ratooning would imply that the one planting had yielded six crops of cane.

In Louisiana cane is planted once in two or three years—rarely is it permitted to remain longer than three years. In Hawaii cane is planted every second year, as a rule, and never goes beyond the single ratooning. Of course, ratoon cane is not so rich, but frequent planting adds tremendously to the expense and necessitates heavy fertilization—however, the increase of yield seems to warrant the outlay, if we may judge from Hawaiian results.

Cuba has some modern plantations and some excellent mills; the cane grown on the island is fairly

SUGAR-MILL AND LABORERS' HOUSES, KEALIA, KAUAI

rich in sucrose, and if it had the same cultivation given cane in Louisiana or in the Hawaiian Islands, yields would be forthcoming, Professor Stubbs estimates, probably as high as five to six tons of sugar to the acre. As it is now, the average Cuban yield is rarely over one to two tons per acre.

According to some sugar-refining experts with whom I have talked on the subject of Hawaiian,

SUGAR-GROWING

Louisianian, and West-Indian sugars—and who have but recently completed a series of exhaustive experiments—the Hawaiian soil is peculiarly suited to cane-growing, and will continue to yield sugar more heavily to the acre than that of Cuba, no matter how scientific the cultivation of soil may become in the latter island, or how complete the machinery for extracting the juice.

Therefore the possibility of sugar-growing becoming unprofitable, and the consequent decadence of the industry in Hawaii, need not concern us—though the day is sure to come when the profits of Hawaiian planters will be materially lessened. They could easily be cut in half and the planters still have handsome returns on the capital invested. However, it will prove a costly mistake if investors feel they cannot lose money in any Hawaiian sugar stock that may be put on the market. It is not unlikely plantations may be floated whose stock will hardly yield satisfactory returns. Hawaii is perhaps destined to undergo one of those characteristically American booms, with an accompanying reaction which will settle hard upon wild plantation schemes that have been launched upon the strength of those already legitimately established.

It will be for Hawaii's best interest if the islands escape one of these booms that fill towns with hungry mechanics and unscrupulous promoters.

CHAPTER XI

COFFEE-PLANTING

EVERY other Hawaiian views the coffee industry as second in importance only to sugar, although in point of fact rice has held for years that place on the export list. Yet it is perfectly true that while rice-growing is standing still, if indeed not decreasing, the production of coffee is rapidly increasing. For example, in 1892 the exportation of rice amounted to eleven and one-half million pounds; in 1894 it had fallen to less than eight million pounds; in 1896, five million; and in 1897 it rose to five and one-half million, all of which was shipped to San Francisco. During that same time coffee, which was eighth on the list, with 13,568 pounds exported in 1892, was fourth in 1894, with 189,150 pounds; in 1896 the export amounted to 255,655 pounds, and in 1897 coffee stood third on the list, with 337,158 pounds—99.62 per cent. of which, by-the-way, came to America. This is a somewhat notable showing, considering the prolonged depression in the industry elsewhere — especially in South America, due to over-production.

A COFFEE CLEARING

COFFEE-PLANTING

Coffee is the newest of Hawaiian industries, and has not yet outgrown the tentative period, with noisy enthusiasts busily proclaiming surety of financial success. Really the industry needs no touting, for its cultivation affords one of the few business opportunities for the migrating settler of smaller means. In fact, it seems about the only field likely, for six months at least, to attract immigration, which will lead to the cutting up and settling of those great tracts of jungle on the island of Hawaii.

Ten years, I believe, is about the present age of Hawaiian coffee-growing under systematic cultivation (though coffee was grown forty years ago casually by individuals), and Kona district on the leeward side of Hawaii, and later Puna district on the same island, were the only ones until very recent years where the industry received intelligent attention. Indeed, until within five years, or thereabouts, Hawaii was the only island believed congenial to the plant; though that seems passing strange, considering it had never been tried on any of the other islands, and that trees were growing wild on Molokai. The conclusion, however, was characteristic of the native.

Because it came originally from that district, Hawaiian coffee was first known in the market as Kona coffee, and as such achieved an enviable reputation, and a price somewhat above that commanded by the best products of Central and South

America. Indeed, up to this writing, no coffee has been yet produced in other districts of the Hawaiian Islands that experts consider equal in flavor to that coming from the original district.

Undoubtedly Kona's location, peculiarly favoring coffee cultivation, has much to do with the flavor of its berry. Kona is on the leeward side of Hawaii, and therefore completely sheltered from the trade-winds—a most important matter, since wind is the blight of the coffee-shrub. The country is rough, the soil of volcanic origin—decomposed and very rich—and the climate, with its wet and dry seasons, more favoring, apparently, on this side of the island than on the other, or windward, where the separation of the seasons is not so distinct. Those learned in coffee-culture claim that a climate characterized by wet and dry seasons is quite essential to the very best results. But this is more or less speculation, so far as Hawaii is concerned, since the plantations on the windward side have not attained the age to make comparison with Kona, on the other side, fair; while, at their present stage of development, the greater abundance of rain appears to have had no appreciably harmful effect.

Speculation, in truth, rules in most of the discussions anent the coffee industry in these more or less experimental days; for, though the export has been increasing year by year, and the industry spreading largely, none the less there is no settled

TOPPED PLANTS AND PLANTATION LABORERS

COFFEE-PLANTING

dictum, such as obtains in the sugar or rice industries. For instance, there is division of opinion as to whether the coffee-trees should be kept cut down to a certain height, or permitted to grow rank; whether the plantation should be entirely cleared of its forest, or enough left to shade the coffee-bushes; whether the shrubs do better at a comparatively low elevation—twelve hundred feet or under —or whether they should range at elevations between twelve hundred and two thousand feet. And there are many other mooted questions the coffee-planters of Hawaii are worrying over, which only time will answer.

Elsewhere experience differs—in India some of the most successful plantations are at a comparatively high elevation, while in the Malay Peninsula the best-looking ones I saw were at a comparatively low elevation. In Kona itself are splendid-looking pieces of coffee between two thousand and twenty-five hundred feet above the sea, and a number of coffee clearings at that elevation were being made in the country through which I rode going from Hilo towards the Kilauea volcano. The bean of coffee grown at the higher elevation is usually larger, but, on the other hand, the crop of trees planted lower matures several months earlier.

Yet another question on which there is much division of opinion is the proper distance at which the coffee-shrubs should be planted one from the other. In India the trees are topped at about four

HAWAIIAN-AMERICA

feet, and six feet allowed between every two; in Central America and on the majority of South-American plantations trees are set out nine feet apart and allowed to grow their natural height; on the Malay Peninsula the trees are topped, as a rule, and set out about six feet apart.

Until Hawaiian planters have had at least another five years' experience, speculation will continue a feature of local culture, and each planter must work out his own salvation by the light of his knowledge of the industry and his ability to modify conditions to meet the requirements of a new country. For coffee is a healthful though a fickle shrub, exceedingly susceptible to altering conditions, and requiring skilful, delicate handling —no part of it so much as the topping and pruning of the young trees. Pruning coffee-trees is an art which obtains to increase the productiveness of the tree, and not for its ornamentation — as we trim hedges and mar fir-trees. With those who believe in topping, the proper age at which the trees should be cut down to the desired height (which may vary from three and a half to five feet) is from eighteen months to two years.

The idea ignorantly but frequently held regards this trimming done so the crop may be the easier picked; but the real reason for topping and pruning is because it increases materially the bearing of the trees through the growing of additional primary and secondary branches. This operation,

COFFEE-PLANTING

so important to the success of the plantation, must be performed with great care and persistency, and the inability to secure skilled labor, and the difficulty of training the inexperienced, are just now among the severest trials of Hawaiian coffee-planters—themselves none too well versed in the scientific requirements of the industry.

The nursery stage is even more exacting. And here also we find a division of opinion and varying methods in Hawaii. Formerly, in more amateurish days, the young plants which sprout up under old coffee-trees were used almost entirely for new plantings, and in many cases where the selection was careful and somewhat learned the results were excellent. But in many more cases not over sixty per cent., to make a generous estimate, resulted happily. Those who study coffee-culture deeply are agreed that long-lived or vigorous trees cannot be produced from the average plant of this description, and that the only dependable, practical way of procuring healthful plants is by raising them in a nursery from seed carefully chosen.

But the coffee nursery is the most sensitive of nurseries, requiring constant intelligent care, and such patience as only a long-suffering character of biblical history is said to have possessed. The nursery may be costly, too, though not usually, that being a matter regulated by conditions of land and environment. The three essentials are: first—adequate water-supply; second—a soil at least eighteen inches deep and entirely free of roots, etc.; third—artificial shade for the seedlings, which must not interfere with the work of care-takers, and that may

A NURSERY

be removed altogether when the need of it has passed—for at a proper age the plants are gradually submitted to the sun, and for a few months before transplanting are quite unshaded.

COFFEE-PLANTING

It is a plant of many and various moods, and requires a lot of knowing in the cultivator.

The amount of coffee the first crop will yield is another one of those questions too puzzling for uncertain Hawaiian experience. Mr. Charles D. Miller, who is preparing a work on coffee-culture, and to whom I am indebted for many figures given herewith, says that, judged by his experience, a return of one pound per tree may be looked for the third year. At maturity — *i.e.*, in the seventh year — the plantation will yield from one and one-half to two pounds to the tree.

BRANCH OF COFFEE-BUSH, SHOWING BERRY

These figures are really approximate, for the industry is too young to permit of unquestionable statistics. I saw some trees

—a great many, in fact—that bore three and four pounds each. It is simple enough to estimate the bearing of a tree if one has time and patience to count the clusters, and the berries in one cluster, and knows that, according to elevation, it takes from nine to twelve hundred berries to make one pound of clean coffee.

The very wisest thing the Hawaiian planters have done is employment of the proper machinery for curing the crop and placing the coffee on the market at its best. Perhaps nothing is more essential to the success of coffee than proper curing and grading—by way of emphasizing which a practical illustration may be given: A few years ago, before the Hawaiian planters had attained the wisdom born of experience, their coffee went on to the market badly mixed, and eighteen cents per pound was the highest price received for the very best; so soon as the proper machinery was put in and the coffee cleaned and graded, the very same berry that had fetched only eighteen cents commanded twenty-five. The coffee of the Malay Peninsula has suffered a great disadvantage in being put on the London market improperly graded, and the industry on the peninsula has languished because of it.

No coffee leaves the island of Hawaii without having undergone the proper and modern processes. The island planters had their lesson, and profited by it. The needed machinery is not very expensive, and consequently, besides quasi-public curing-plants, many planters have their own, and frequently several planters use one in partnership. The process consists of pulping the berry and washing and curing and grading the bean; dry hulling the

PLANTS SHADED BY CASTOR-BEANS

bean is not so favorably regarded as the washing process.

No doubt the Hawaiian Islands are destined in a very few years to export several hundred per cent. more coffee than the returns of last year show; in time possibly coffee may become a good second to sugar in the annual exports. Certainly coffee is the industry which is going to settle up the islands, especially Hawaii, and be the means of securing more reasonable transportation rates than now obtain. Coffee will be the means, too, of attracting that desirable class of immigrant—the man of comparatively small capital—seeking a home where he may invest his money.

There is some coffee-land on all the islands, but Hawaii is the only one of the group that has land for public settlement. This is true of other industries than coffee. The principal coffee districts in the island of Hawaii are—Kona, 48,000 acres; Puna, 67,000 acres; and Hilo, 195,000 acres; but a comparatively small percentage of this acreage is planted with coffee or suitable to its cultivation. In all three of these districts, and especially in Hilo, the government is surveying and opening land for settlement as rapidly as possible. And as fast as the land is put on the market it is being taken up; for the government sells it from five to ten dollars an acre, while the boom at the town of Hilo—Hawaii—enables speculators to get fifty, sixty, and even one hundred dollars an acre for the same land, and about thirty to forty dollars an acre must be reckoned on additionally for clearing off the dense jungle and forest.

Careful figuring counts the cost of caring for a coffee-plantation at from $150 to $200 per acre for five years. There is a comparatively small quantity of land for outright sale—nearly all the desirable

COFFEE-PLANTING

land on all the islands is owned or held under long leases, some of them so long as thirty years, which is the limit of life of the coffee-tree under cultivation. On Maui, Kauai, and a little on Oahu, coffee has been planted, and prospects reported "flattering," but only on Hawaii have there as yet been results tangible enough to give an idea of possible profits. Taking a fair average of success at this stage of the industry, a conservative estimate on the commencement of the fifth year places the profit at fifteen to twenty per cent. on the original investment. The Waianai plant (Oahu) paid for itself in six years, and last year produced sixteen tons of coffee besides.

Fortunately, on none of the islands has any species of blight made its appearance.

Coffee-planters further purpose setting out bananas on their coffee-fields, thus making the soil do twofold service without injury to either crop, and yield double profit to the grower; half a ton of coffee and three hundred branches of bananas an acre, as confidently expected from good average soil, would not prove a bad return. The coffee boom is on in the island of Hawaii, and so fast as the government opens new roads into the coffee-belts, and plots public land for settlement, just so fast is it being taken up. I trust the Hawaiians will have sense enough not to dip too deeply into the boom business. Values have been greatly enhanced and prospects brightened through the assurance of stable

HAWAIIAN-AMERICA

government given by annexation, but undue inflation will do more harm than good to the country.

UNTRIMMED TREES, ABOUT THREE YEARS OLD

Investors will bear in mind that land devoid of tree-growth should be viewed with suspicion; while where guavas or lantana or the tree-ferns are found it is pretty safe to judge the soil suitable to coffee. And if it lies in the zone of a wet and a dry season, so much the better, for so may the planter harvest his crop within a limited period, thus diminishing the cost of picking, and giving him the opportunity to cure his crop by sun, which is not so costly and does not demand the skill or machinery required by the artificial methods necessary to the very wet countries.

Above all else, there must be shelter from wind.

CHAPTER XII

GAMES AND FEASTS

IN the old days there were many games demanding vigorous skill, for the native appears to have been a sportsman of courage and originality. One of the most popular diversions of the sporting *alii* (nobility) was shark-killing, and the procedure was as unique among recreations as it appears to have been diverting. An unfortunate of the common people, who had perhaps broken *tabu*, or permitted his shadow to fall across the path of a passing chief, or committed one or the other of the indiscretions which merited speedy death in the ancient Hawaiian days, was killed, and his body cut into pieces and placed upon a wooden tray similar to that used for serving roast pig.

The tray, with its shivering, crimson-stained bait, was then set out in the sun, and when it had reached the stage of decomposition that permitted of no uncertainty as to its location even on the blackest night, it had become the most tempting of shark lures.

And now the final, and no doubt most exciting,

stage of the sport began. With much ceremony, and some inclination (on the part of the less hardy) to keep to windward, the Lucullian feast, still on its platter, was conveyed beyond the reef, and there, while quite a flotilla of canoes gathered for the sport, set afloat upon the pellucid waters.

Sharks were plentiful in Hawaiian waters beyond the reefs, and the odor of the savory bait was very fetching, therefore the sport usually began promptly. As soon as the voracious fish seized the bait, the natives, armed with stout knives and daggers made of stone, and sometimes of shark's teeth, dove into the water and attacked them. From the furious battle which resulted the native almost invariably emerged unharmed.

Perhaps there are no people on earth more thoroughly at home in the water than the Hawaiians — men and women; and though civilization has lessened their opportunity for indulgence, yet it has not diminished their amphibious tendencies. One of the old sports which remains to keep alive native skill, and in modified form to captivate every foreigner who tries it, is surf-riding. It may, in fact, be called the national sport of Hawaii, and formerly the youth took great pride in their skill and daring. Nowadays it has lost its former great vogue among natives, and the *onini*

SLED

(surf-board) gives place almost invariably to the canoe.

The *onini* is a board made of the famous *koa* wood, about twelve to eighteen inches wide and from six to eight feet long, often with flat surface, but usually with both sides slightly rounded. Pushing the boards before them, the natives swim beyond the breakers, where they await the approach of a suitable incoming wave; when one sufficiently large is seen, they lie on the board face downward, and paddle with hands and feet shoreward, until the wave overtakes them, when by expert manipulation the *onini* is kept on the face of the wave and carried towards the beach at steamboat speed. As the board rests on the face of the wave at a considerable angle, some idea may be had of the skill required to keep it there during the quarter-mile rush for the shore. And yet some of the natives become so expert that they stand upon the board during the steadier periods of its flight.

Surf-riding in a canoe sounds tame after this; but it really is not. There is precisely the same procedure, the identical sensations, and indeed I am of half a mind that greater skill is required to hold the larger, clumsier canoe on the face of the wave than the lighter, handier *onini*.

The advantage of the canoe is the opportunity it offers for gregarious enjoyment. The Hawaiian canoe of to-day is of the type used in the days of Kamehameha the Great; it has not altered in model

a particle, and with good reason, for it could not be improved on for Hawaii's open waterways. It is a dugout, fairly deep and narrow, with bow and stern starboard outriggers about five feet long, to which at the farthermost outward end is attached a fairly large, round (about six inches in diameter), but very buoyant spar that is about three-quarters the length of the canoe. With this rig the canoes go through rather rough water; and the fact that in the early days the natives cruised from one island to another in them rather indorses their seaworthiness. The paddles are somewhat long and stout, with very short, wide blades, adapted to rough, open-water work.

There must be at least a couple of strong paddlers, and a helmsman of experience and skill in surf-riding, else the canoe will be swamped at once. Oftentimes the surf is running high and makes the outgoing exciting, but the canoe is taken well out before turning to wait for a wave large enough to assure a carry to the shore. Several waves are permitted to pass perhaps before a big one is sighted three hundred yards away, and then—"*Hoi! hoi!*" (Paddle! paddle!) cries the helmsman, and desperate, quick strokes send the canoe forward at a rattling pace, which must be maintained until the wave overtakes the boat. If the canoe has not pace enough, the wave swamps it and rolls on towards shore, leaving a capsized party in its wake. But if not overwhelmed, there comes, immediately on the wave picking up the canoe, the most thrilling sensation you have ever experienced.

Paddling like mad, your back towards the sea, you have not seen the wave drawing nearer and nearer. Suddenly the canoe is lifted, without shock, and carried forward at great speed, and you know you are at least successfully launched in the great native sport. In front, the bow, cutting the water, sends strings of spray backward and upward; at the stern, the great blue-green wall curls above and over you, and if you are a sentient creature your pulse thrills with an exhilaration that no other sport in my experience can supply. It is tobogganing without its gasping, blinding speed.

Always the steersman must be on the alert, for the incoming wave has many eccentricities, and often the desperate paddling must be resorted to for a few moments at a time to avoid being capsized. The canoe must be kept on the face of the wave or it will be quickly overwhelmed.

Next to surf-riding, the most honored of ancient Hawaiian sports was hill-coasting on long, narrow sledges. It would seem impossible that any speed could be made under the conditions, and yet abundant evidence exists to prove it. The course, made of dry grass and smooth stones, was laid down the side of a steep hill, and the pace attained sent the coaster quite a distance across the plain at the foot of the runway. I noted these old courses in my travels over the islands, very

NATIVE WRESTLERS

plainly marking several precipitous hill-sides, and suggesting a considerable amount of toil in their original making. The sledge was only six inches wide by three inches deep, and about twelve feet long, made very stoutly, and of hard wood.

Hill-coasting must have been somewhat of an expensive sport, suited only to the *alii*.

But the favorite recreations of the common people, perhaps, were the use of the slung-shot and the throwing of several kinds of darts. These darts were from two to five feet in length, of various diameters, and made very neatly of hard wood. The native is said to have been very dexterous in throwing them—sometimes between upright posts, sometimes against a target, sometimes along the ground, and always with much force and accuracy. A similar game was hurling and catching and returning or warding off a javelin, made also of hard wood. As the javelin was the chief weapon of war, this game was fostered by the *alii*, and tournaments where the dependants of the chiefs met in rivalry were of frequent occurrence. Ancient Hawaiians are credited with being very expert in hurling darts and javelins, and in dodging them.

Then there was a game somewhat on the order of bowling, which must have necessitated long practice to acquire skill. It consisted of hurling a highly polished stone disk, about three inches in diameter and one inch and a half thick, through two sticks separated only a few inches, and from one hundred and fifty to two hundred feet from the starting-line. Another form of the game was hurling the disk for a distance along a prepared course—a mere test of strength. These disks were usually made of lava, very carefully cared for and highly prized.

Wrestling and foot-racing were other sports more general among the common people; and the ancient and simple manner of the former continues to this day—viz., the two contestants stand facing; each clasps the other's hands, fingers interlaced, and, at the word, strives, without unclasping hands or touching other parts of the body, to put the other off the mat. The one first to be pushed off the mat loses the bout.

Boxing was confined largely to the *alii*, was very severe in method, and the exhibitions were considered most important sporting events. Frequently rural chiefs decided friendly, and sometimes unfriendly, disputes in the ring, and the days of contests marked a veritable gathering of the clans, which often indulged in unrestrained and partisan demonstrations. Sometimes a contestant was killed, and then a general mêlée resulted.

Of the less athletic games there were quite a number: one, a kind of checkers with black and white stones on a board marked off in squares; another —and what I believe must be the original shell-game of modern notoriety—consisted in hiding a small stone under one of several pieces of *kapa* (native cloth) and guessing on its location. Hawaiians were, like most aborigines, inveterate gamblers, and employed all these games in the gratification of their passion.

But perhaps the Hawaiians of the old days, and of comparatively modern days, have always gotten most entertainment from their dancing and singing. Not that either is entrancing, but their music certainly is melodious, and their dancing as interesting as any of the Far Eastern types—Japanese, Siamese, Malay—which all consist of mere posturing.

The dance of Hawaii is the *hula-hula*, which originally consisted of a series of mild muscular contortions of harmless intent, made to the more or less mournful accompaniment of prolonged and monotonous chants on primitive drums, rattles, and flute. After a time, and during the latter years of the monarchy especially, the lewd possibilities of the dance and the naturally lustful nature of the natives changed the character of the *hula-hula* to indecent posturing done to the accompaniment of lascivious songs.

During Kalakaua's reign, for instance, a *hula-hula* implied women dancing practically naked and a night of gin and general dissipation. Those days, however, departed with Kalakaua's death. The dance thrives these days chiefly to satisfy the curiosity of tourists, who pay ridiculous prices in the hope of seeing something devilish—and are usually greatly disappointed. The *hula-hula* is a cross between a coochee-coochee and a Highland fling, and has suggestive possibilities, but ordinarily it is of the Eastern type and rather stupid.

Dearest to the native's heart, however—dearer than the *hula-hula* or singing—is the *luan*, which is Hawaiian for feast, and frequently comprehensive enough to include all manner of post-prandial entertainment.

In Honolulu almost any dinner is called a *luan*, at which there are guests, and where the table is decorated with flowers and *poi* served. One must go into the country, however, to get an idea of what the real *luan* is, and even so, at best, there are foreign and incongruous adjuncts. The native has become too civilized to drop into even the old pleasures with familiarity. At all events, the country imitation is an improvement on that of the town, where often there are tables and chairs and many other modern utensils.

The table of the country is a mat of fine braiding laid on the ground and richly decorated with ferns and *maile*—the Hawaiian smilax—and garlands of many different flowers. At each one's place are *leis* (wreaths to be put about the neck or around the hat) of tuberoses, or golden *ilimas*, or carnations—red, white, and pink. There are no knives, forks, or spoons, and the dishes are calabashes of brilliantly polished *koa*, or shiny cocoanut shells, or small gourds. The average foreigner will not enjoy many of the prepared dishes, but he will

HULA-HULA GIRLS IN DANCING COSTUME

GAMES AND FEASTS

be sure to find the fish steamed in *ti* leaves toothsome, and ready to declare the pork roasted in an underground oven the most delicious in his epicurean experience. Another dish he will enjoy is a salad of alligator-pear, and he may even relish the

A *LUAU* IN THE COUNTRY

squid, as dry octopus tentacles are called, though the various kinds of raw delicacies he will pass. But the real delicacy of Hawaii and other semi-tropical countries is the green cocoanut, eaten out of the shell. Pink *poi* and baked taro usually form the background of these feasts. If there is anything to drink, it will be beer or gin.

With the exception of surf-riding, all the old games have passed, and in their stead have come the several varieties of modern sport. There is an athletic association, a bicycle-track, a rifle association, a yacht club with many boats, and a rowing association of three clubs. The various schools annually put forth baseball and football teams, and the native takes well to both games. In track athletics there is less development, and what there is is chiefly confined to Hawaiians of white parentage.

The native pure and simple takes more kindly to boating, and, in fact, so does all Hawaii, for holidays are made of the annual yacht regatta and boat-club race-days. Moreover, the rowing form is surprisingly good, nearly equal to the average shown by American boat-club crews. Plover, snipe, and ducks may be found on all the islands, and furnish very good sport; and a species of wild-goose peculiar to Hawaii formerly abounded, but is now practically extinct.

On most of the islands, too, are goats and pigs, originally domestic, which have run wild for many years and multiplied, especially the goats, and that furnish sport for the rifle, in view of nothing better. It is rather good fun, if you are well mounted, to run down the hogs, and pig-sticking could be easily introduced; but Hawaiians use revolvers. The pigs differ from the Indian, or Malayan, or European wild variety, and look more like the common barn-yard hog, though their tushes grow long, and they are speedy, and on occasion vicious.

On the island of Molokai are large herds of the little spotted deer which was introduced from China many years ago, and has thrived greatly. But there is no more sport killing one of these than there is in summer in killing the herds of Barren Ground caribou, which in the hot season seek the lakes of the lower country, and will pass in countless hundreds within fifty yards of you.

There are no other game animals—no other wild animals, indeed. Hawaii is singularly lacking in natural fauna—rats, mice, dogs, and cats only are indigenous, and were all eaten in the old days, and —blessed country for camping—there are no reptiles, no venomous insects, only a few centipedes, spiders, and scorpions.

Bird life is scarce, too, and growing more so. The Oo and Mamo, that furnished the yellow feathers for the famous cloaks of Hawaiian royalty, were found only on the islands of Hawaii and Kauai, but have now almost disappeared. There are few birds to enliven the forests, and really none in the lowlands save the saucy sparrow Myna, the impudent fellow of India. The angling is all in the sea, and the varieties of fish many, with one or two which furnish good sport.

CHAPTER XIII

EDUCATING THE NATIVE

ONE of the local issues to which the Honolulu visitor first becomes alive is the pro and anti missionary feeling, with decided opinions on all island subjects in absolute though mild confliction. The missionary element of Hawaii needs no defender. Its splendid work speaks for itself. The pioneer missionaries set upon their labor of civilization with intelligence, and their descendants have carried it on with kindness and judgment as part of their inheritance. From father to son and from son to son the work has been passed along not only in the church, but in the social, industrial, educational life of the natives.

It is the missionary element that has educated these natives of Hawaii, checked their destroying thirst for drink, and cleansed their minds and bodies.

The descent of the missionaries upon Hawaii and the beginning of native education were coeval. Therefore this chapter would be incomplete without some reference to the pioneers who began the

EDUCATING THE NATIVE

work which in seventy years has raised the people of these islands from lowest degradation to a condition of average literacy higher than that of all other countries save the United States, Prussia, and Switzerland, and to a wealth *per capita* averaging greater than any other country in the world. By way of emphasizing that statement — Hawaii's wealth *per capita*, on its population of (about) 100,000, is $60; that of the United States, on a basis of 72,000,000 population, is $23 70.

The first company of missionaries for Hawaii started from Boston in the brig *Thaddeus* in 1819— by strange coincidence the very year in which the Hawaiians of their own volition abandoned idolatry. The party included Asa Thurston and Hiram Bringham, just graduated from the Andover Theological Seminary; Samuel Whitney and Samuel Ruggles, teachers; Elisha Loomis, a printer; Thomas Holman, a physician; Daniel Chamberlain, a farmer; and several Hawaiian young men, whom whaling-ships had brought to America and some of the church people had educated. They reached Honolulu in 1820, and a more auspicious year could hardly have been chosen for the beginning of their labors.

The Hawaiians are an emotional, fickle people, naturally religious, always credulous; having the previous year abandoned their own faith, they were in frame of mind best suited to receive the newcomers. Nevertheless, although many submitted to the Christian doctrine, their conversion the first ten years was not what the circumstances and knowledge of native character would suggest. Perhaps nothing happened in the first years of missionary endeavors that had so powerful and favorable an influence in Christianizing the people as Kapiolani's conversion in 1825. She was a woman *alii* of high rank, living at Kaiwaaloa, near where Captain Cook was killed, and, "getting religion," made a trip to the volcano Kilauea, where, in the presence of many of her kind, she defied the dreaded Pele (goddess of fire) to do her injury.

Her return unharmed was a potent argument for the new faith.

In 1822, John Pickering, of Boston, furnished the basis for a Hawaiian alphabet, and forthwith the first spelling-book for the native was printed by Mr. Loomis. Three years later the leading Hawaiian chiefs adopted the Ten Commandments, and recognized Sunday as a day of rest and worship. But though they subscribed to the Commandments, and passed a law forbidding women to visit ships for immoral purposes, the lust of the native was inherent and too near his heart to permit respect of the Seventh Commandment. Moreover, missionary labors were increased tenfold by attempted protection of native virtue. Since first foreign ships had called at Hawaiian ports, illicit sexual traffic had been no small part of the trade with the islands. Women were sent for so soon as the anchor

EDUCATING THE NATIVE

was cast, if indeed they had not already swum out to meet the incoming ship. And it was by no means a cumpulsory or one-sided traffic.

However, the work of education progressed. In six years after their landing the missionaries had

KAMEHAMEHA BOYS' SCHOOL

secured the assistance of 180 native teachers; in another four years, or in the first ten years of the missionaries' work, 900 schools taught by natives were established, 44,895 scholars attending, and by 1840 care of the schools established by the missionaries was taken over by the government, which from pagan despotism had become a constitutional monarchy. In 1850 a decree was issued setting aside for educational purposes one-twentieth of the public lands; and by 1853, $903,000 had been spent in Christianizing and educating the Hawaiians. Thereafter the churches became and have always continued self-supporting.

Two schools at present existing date their beginning from the earliest of Hawaii's educational period: the seminary of Lahainaluna (Maui), which combines academical instruction with industrial and manual training, established in 1831, and Oahu College, at Honolulu, the development of a school established in 1841, and originally intended by the missionaries for their own children.

In 1865 the Hawaiian Legislature organized the public school system of the country on the lines which, with very few changes, are in use to-day, and instituted a board of education. In 1895 this board was raised from a bureau of the government to the rank of an executive department, with the Minister of Foreign Affairs as *ex-officio* Minister of Public Instruction, and six commissioners, appointed at large, constituting a board with full control of all the public educational interests. To-day there are 192 schools in the islands, employing 507 teachers, with an annual pay-roll of $190,700, and 14,522 pupils. Besides which is a kindergarten system doing inestimable service, and two Young Men's Christian Association buildings—one for the whites and one for the Chinese.

And thus has developed and prospered the edu-

EDUCATING THE NATIVE

cational seed sown by these first missionaries over seventy years ago.

Apart from the united effort and individual loyalty of the actual laborers in the cause, this noteworthy showing is to be attributed to the fact that for the past fifty of those years the educational policy has been a settled one, adhered to persistently, and followed diligently and systematically. Not even in the troublous times of sporadic revolution has there been deviation from the prescribed course.

Education in Hawaii is universal, compulsory, and free.

There are two classes of schools—the government, or free, schools, and the private or independent, or pay, schools. The law of Hawaii makes it obligatory upon all children between the ages of six and fifteen years to attend school regularly, and as the government therefore assumes this educational responsibility, it exercises a certain supervision over private schools, although it does not directly control them.

Until recent years the government schools were of two classes — the "select," or English schools, presided over in large part by American teachers, though a number of the teachers were Hawaiian, of either pure or mixed blood; and the "common," or native, school, where all the teachers were natives, and the language exclusively Hawaiian. From time to time these "common" schools have been replaced by English, at the request of the natives, who in former days invariably, when they could afford it, patronized "select" rather than the "common" schools. There always has been manifest a native disposition to acquire familiarity with the English language.

Gradually the "common" schools were closed out and replaced by English, until to-day there is but one of the former in the land, and at the wish of the natives themselves the language of the islands is English.

There are of course defects in the system, which will be remedied as Hawaii secures larger revenue. There is need of higher scholarship among teachers, of improvement in the system of inspection, of repair to many of the government school-houses. Honolulu, especially in this respect, has outgrown its educational plant. And this is not written in spirit of captious criticism — we must consider the conditions and judge of the results, and certainly nowhere else in the world have similar results been attained. The scholarship average of the English-speaking native is of course quite low, and will no doubt continue so for a generation; the half-white or part Hawaiian is more ambitious, and achieves fairly thorough grounding in the elementary courses that comprise public-school education.

The institutions most importantly concerned in the native's immediate future, however, are the normal and the industrial schools. The former is

EDUCATING THE NATIVE

proving valuable in raising the scholarship of the native and half-white teachers sent into the rural districts, and bettering their system of instruction.

There is no education so serviceable to the native as that which teaches him to utilize for his best advantage the agricultural opportunities which surround him—though I am bound to say he is very

PUNAHOU COLLEGE

slow to do so. Therefore the industrial schools must fill a most important place in Hawaii's educational development.

There are two—the government institution at Maui, to which I have already alluded, and the Kamehameha schools at Honolulu, founded and endowed by Princess Bernice Bishop, descendant of the Kamehamehas. There have been no impressive results from either of these, primarily because the native is slow to take hold of anything that suggests labor, and, secondly, because until within two years or so the methods employed were not so practicable as the field needed.

Formerly the course in the farming department began and ended in pulling weeds, or in digging rocks, or in the desultory care of cows and pigs. Recently, at Kamehameha, a graduate of an American agricultural college has been put in charge of the farming department, and a proper course entered upon that will include tilling the soil, care of stock, and management of a dairy. The course extends over six years, and includes practical instruction in tailoring, printing, wood-turning, blacksmithing, carpentry, and machinery. There are accommodations in this school for about 300 boys, and there are in attendance 130, which is a sufficient commentary on the native's desire for serious work. On the other hand, the fact that 40 out of the 130 are earning their way through the school (the annual expense being only $43) is in a measure a sign of encouragement.

The girls' division of the Kamehameha schools devotes itself to elementary education, and to sewing, house-work, and the like. The native girl — who, by-the-way, has improved more than the native boy — very rarely, however, goes out to domestic service, and the hope of these schools lies in the missionary work pupils may

KAMEHAMEHA GIRLS' SCHOOL

do among their people after they have been graduated.

There are, besides, half a dozen boarding-schools, where, in addition to the ordinary school course, girls are receiving training in cooking and civilized modes of living.

The Honolulu High School was established in 1895, to help supply the growing need for academies giving more advanced instruction. Oahu college is quartered in handsome buildings surrounded by beautiful grounds, has an efficient staff, and all the needed equipment for a college of its size.

The Reform School is another of decided practicability, which gives boys the ordinary studies prescribed by the government schools, in addition to instructing them in harness-making and cabinet-work, and in making the simpler articles of tinware and their own clothing. Then there is a night-school, which serves the twofold purpose of teaching English to those who have arrived in the country (like the Portuguese, for instance) beyond the day-school age, and provides opportunity for that small class which has had its ordinary schooling and gone to work with ambition for further learning.

But the kindergartens, which are supported by public charity, it seems to me are among the most beneficial in the general betterment of these people. It is beginning at the very beginning — the only intelligent starting-point for the semi-civilized. It is a great philanthropic venture against the curse of pauperism. Education is the antidote of pauperism; the kindergarten is therefore the first barrier against indigence and crime and intemperance.

At Honolulu there are kindergartens for all nationalities — Chinese, Japanese, Hawaiian, English — and a magnificent work is being done that will begin most to satisfactorily reveal itself in another two or three years. Already there is much evidence of its beneficial working.

Instruction in a foreign tongue that tends to real enlightenment, genuine education — the education that prompts better thinking and better feeling — is a weighty problem. And the instructors of Hawaii have found it equally as puzzling as have those who have undertaken the civilization of other uncivilized people. The natives of the Hawaiian Islands have adopted the white man's religion with unexampled rapidity and universality. They have learned to at least read and write in their own language so generally that those of the population under forty years of age signing their names with a cross are rarely met, and some few have learned to read and write the English language. But the learning has been purely of the mechanical kind, as quite naturally it would be at this stage.

Few of those who at fifteen quit school have ac-

LUNALILO HOME FOR AGED AND INDIGENT NATIVES

quired any idea of English literature in its simplest forms, or of the significance of education, and about as few have acquired a taste or habit for reading that will tend to increase their intelligence. Yet of course there have been a few exceptions. I speak only of the generality. The native Hawaiian is not naturally an apt pupil. His mind is not alert, and his disposition is for making the least effort compatible with attaining the obligatory standard, whether it be at school or in the field. And there is nothing surprising in this: tradition, environment, all indicate it. The surprise, to my mind, is that the native should have overcome his natural tendency so much as to permit of his recorded accomplishments.

Education has not made the native Hawaiian industrious—or shall I say more industrious than formerly?—but education has certainly made the present generation honest, more intelligent than the old one, cleaner in body and in mind, and less intemperate. And of these certainly none has had greater influence on the natives' healthier, honester, more intelligent living than the comparative temperance which the prohibition laws and the persistent labor of early missionaries, and their sons after them, have been the means of maintaining.

Perhaps the native never will attain the true significance of education, or acquire literary habits. What matters it, so long as he learns to have purer thoughts and lives more healthfully? What better education could he have, and truly what more does he need?

The days of the native are passing quickly, and if they pass without lettered learning, he is at least leaving the best of his blood and of the education he has acquired in the half-caste, in whom that deeper educational significance seems awakening.

CHAPTER XIV

IN FEUDAL DAYS

THE study of ancient Hawaii yields little that is impressive. Few peoples have left less to indicate early prowess, and none has left so few monuments to suggest a period of splendid, if savage, accomplishments. There are no temples of grand proportions and complex architecture, no idols of a fashioning to cause wonder, no relics of an ancient admirable art. They appear always to have been an acquiescent people, with little originality or force of character, and only the industry born of necessity.

Ancient Hawaiians, in truth, created little. Of all the peoples in the southern half of the great Pacific Ocean their handiwork reveals less originality, less art, least diligence. They did no stone-carving equal to that of the Tahitians, nor basket-braiding so good as the Samoans, nor wood-carving to be compared with the remarkable work of the Maoris, or with that of the Fijians. The yellow feather cloaks the Hawaiians made (in comparatively modern times) for royalty certainly represent careful toil, but were notable chiefly for the time consumed in their manufacture, and do not disclose the originality in design or artistic grotesqueness of the birdwork done by the untamed races of New Guinea. Although they were so largely a voyaging people, their canoes were marked with less finish than those of almost any of the Polynesians, and were never

Gourd Drum   Flute   Rattles   Shark-skin Drum
Used in Hula-Hula Dances

MUSICAL INSTRUMENTS

decorated. Indeed, Hawaiian workmanship does not show either the thought in design or skill in execution or decoration of even the Alaskans.

The only arts that really ever flourished in Hawaii were those that made for the manufacture of *Kapa*, the royal bird-feather cloaks, and, to a small extent, baskets.

Kapa was made from the *wauke* and *mamake* inner tree bark, which was first soaked to a pulpy consistency and then beaten out into strong fibrous sheets. Sometimes these sheets were bleached nearly white; sometimes they were decorated in straight or curved lines differently colored by mineral dyes, laid on with bamboo stamps, and invariably glazed with a resinous preparation. The *Kapa* might be beaten into fine sheets, in which case it became the woman's skirt (*pau*), or thicker, it was the man's loin-cloth (*malo*), or the covering during sleep.

The feather cloak was perhaps the most expensive cape that ever hung from royal shoulders; it was made by sewing together many of the countless single tufts of yellow taken from the wing of the Oo, a bird of otherwise black plumage. As the cloaks always hung well below the waist, and not infrequently reached the ground, it may be appreciated how many birds were required in the making of a single cloak, and what patience and time were required to attach these tufts together so closely and so firmly by their respective quills as to give to the completed work the appearance of absolute unity. A helmet worn by the chiefs was made of red feathers from the Mamo, which also furnished a coarser yellow feather used for the royal cloaks when the Oo had later become very scarce; but the shapes of both cloak and helmet were suggested by Spanish models.

Even the calabash, perhaps the best relic of Hawaiian art, did not originate on the Hawaiian Islands. In the old days there were many different shapes and sizes of calabashes, decorated often, and, when large or of the platter shape, made in-

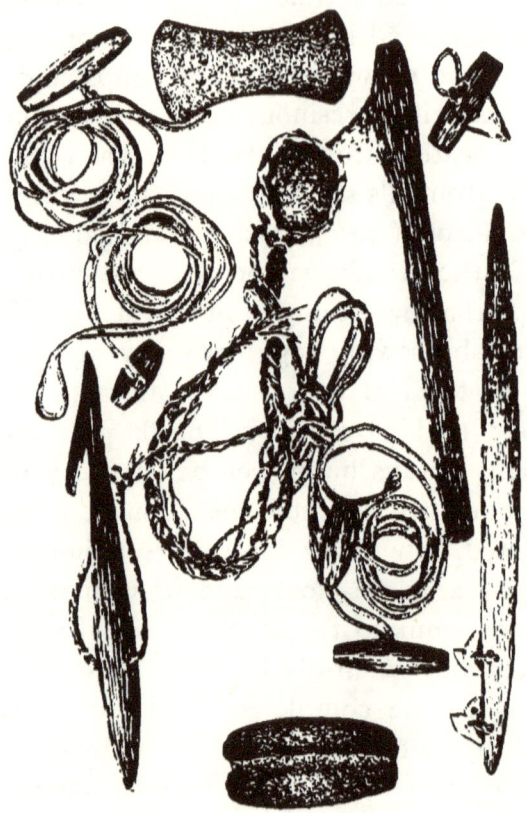

ANCIENT SHARK TOOTH, KNIVES, FISH-HOOKS, AND SLUNG-SHOT

variably of *Koa*—a wood fine of grain and susceptible of beautiful polish. The small calabash, then as now, was frequently made of cocoanut-shell or from a gourd. In common with most islands in the southern Pacific there is no metal on Hawaii, and tools for cutting were therefore either the teeth of sharks or made from stone; considering the crudity of these implements, the results attained were somewhat praiseworthy.

The date of settlement of the Hawaiian Islands, although not authentically established, is usually placed at 500 A.D. As to the date of their discovery there appears also to be some uncertainty, increased greatly by the honor being usually given to Captain James Cook, an English navigator. The most careful historians credit the actual discovery of the islands to a Spanish navigator, Juan Gaetano, in 1555, though apart from bestowing some more or less apt, if fanciful, names upon the islands, the Spaniard made no effort to establish proprietary rights, or to reap trade or other benefits from the discovery. Except for another Spanish navigator, who was wrecked off one of the islands, and with his sister washed ashore—both finally to marry natives of chieftain blood —there is no record of white visitation to Hawaii until Captain Cook's first arrival in January, 1778. Therefore, though the Englishman's was really a rediscovery, he gave them the name Sandwich—in honor of his patron, the first Lord of the English Admiralty and the fourth earl of that house—by which they became known to the world and first brought into contact with the white race, that was to fill so important a place in their development.

But this English rediscovery was really in the days of comparatively modern Hawaii.

Hawaiians have legends of human creation, like many other aborigines, suggestive of tales told by early missionaries and perverted, and they have likewise some rather highly colored stories of the creation of the islands; but their mythology contains little of instruction or interest. It was largely concerned with the baser passions. Their religion was gloomy, and filled with oppressive rites. Idols were abundant, grotesque, and hideous: all to be feared and all to be propitiated. Both men and women were abnormally superstitious, and in supplication sought the gods for every purpose. There were wind gods, poison gods, fire gods; and Pele, the goddess who reigned in the volcano they deified. Strange enough, they had no worship of sun or moon, common to most aborigines; and, strange again, they practised the rite of circumcision until modern times.

Though they were not cannibals—and the story of their eating the flesh of Captain Cook is a fairy tale—yet there was abundant sacrifice of human life. Indeed, life was held very cheaply. On the completion of a new house, or temple of refuge (where one's enemies might not pursue), or the launching of a canoe, or death of a chief, human sacrifice was offered to the insatiable gods. Infanticide prevailed to a very great extent. The flesh was carefully removed from the bones of the deceased and buried, and the bones secretly hidden in a cave or burned, in obedience to the superstitious dread of an enemy securing them, and thereby weaving a spell to their undoing. Later, when they overcame this fear and the dead were buried (always on high places—usually a hill-top), the bodies of priest and chiefs were laid out straight, while those of the common people were buried sitting, in shallow graves. There were no funeral rites, but a burial gave license for all manner of dissipations, usually of a low and bestial order.

They were a fairly courageous people in the mob warfare of their hand-to-hand conflicts, their weapons being usually spears, but as often javelins and clubs, all of hard wood, as well as slings made of cocoa fibre or human hair, with which they hurled stones with considerable accuracy.

WOODEN BASINS INLAID WITH HUMAN BONES AND TEETH

They did not tattoo the bodies like the Samoans, Maoris, Malays, or Siamese, but they slit the ears of men detected of cowardice.

Ancient Hawaii was really divided into three periods: (1) The age of *Menehunes*, as it has been called, or skilled workers. (2) Rise of Feudalism. (3) Beginning of the Monarchy.

The earliest period of Hawaiian history appears, by all accounts, to have been a time of peace and plenty; a veritable golden age, marked by industrial enterprise and prosperity. The population seems to have been much less than is later reported, and arable land and water existed in sufficient quantity for all. There were no selfish chiefs of power to extend their land boundaries beyond fair limit, or place the ban of *tabu* on such fields of taro as caught their greedy eye. The humblest subject might be sure of remaining in undisturbed possession of the works of his industry, and therefore the people prospered. Deep-water fish-ponds, to insure an invariable and somewhat easier catch, were made by building great sea-walls which enclosed small bays near the settlements; irrigating systems were established, and the manufacture of *Kapa* and basket-braiding flourished.

There was no land tenure in this period, although irrigation was slowly developing the principle of it. Possession and use decided the right to holdings, and as water was plentiful enough for all to use it freely, no occasion arose for laws more intricate. As the population increased, however, and the richer land grew scarce, irrigation became necessary in order to reclaim the less fertile soil. And with irrigation, and the consequent toil it involved in ditch-building, grading, etc., came increased value of land and accompanying need of a clearer sense of ownership, based upon the investment of labor which the soil demanded.

Although it is natural to suppose disputes over land boundaries arose, and, no doubt, occasional feuds, yet the period appears to have been notably free from scenes of violence generally, or even in individual cases. Tribal government and land tenure, based on possession and cultivation of the soil, evidently ruled for many generations: and land passed from father to son on this very fair principle of ownership. Increasing population, however, with the consequent lessening of more desirable lands and the expanding value of those under cultivation, created in the community a disturbing element which spread with rapidity, and developed malignity as it spread.

And so in the middle of the thirteenth century the feudal days began, and a period of turbulence set in that interrupted peaceful industry and destroyed many of the works which had been builded with such care and patience. Internecine warfare was declared, and the soil neglected; each island was distracted by the conflicts of its several powerful chiefs each with his retinue, each striving for greater authority and aggrandizement. It was impossible for any one to remain aloof: all the people were at war from the very necessity of attaching themselves to a given standard for the protection of life it afforded.

As a chief won, his power grew; so in the course of time, and through a survival of the fittest procedure, it came about that one high chief practically ruled on each island, with a number of petty chiefs, who in turn had their leaders and separate retinues of followers, and all of these, on various and frequent occasions, were united in a common cause or divided into various factions, as interest and number prompted.

Thus it happened that at this time, in the century of Captain Cook's coming, the people of Hawaii were divided into three classes—the *Alii*, or nobles, which included the high chiefs and their sub-chiefs; the *Kahunas*, or priests, the learned class, who were greatly respected by the people, whom they often aided against the oppression of the *Alii*; and the *Makaainana*, or common people, who at this period, and until the rise of white influence, were serfs, holding nothing secure from their immediate chief, not even their own lives.

Might ruled in the social as it did in the political system. There was no law of marriage; the number of women in a household was limited only by the temperament and power of the master; and women members of the *Alii* had the privilege, not enjoyed by their humbler sisters, of similar indulgence in the matter of connubial partners. Hawaiians, however, are a pleasing exception among aborigines in not making of their womankind a family beast of burden; in fact, the woman of Hawaii may be called the aboriginal new woman. She enjoyed the chief's confidence and shared his counsel, chose her own husband or husbands, and gave rank and lineage to the child. There is no family name in Hawaii, and the christian name of the child may have no relation to that of its father.

A most elaborate system of *tabu* existed, and was operated by the *Alii* for their full and material benefit. If a chief wanted a field of *taro* that particularly pleased his eye, he had but to set up a pole in its midst with a flag of white *Kapa* attached, and the field was his and *tabu* to the toiling cultivator; if the chief desired unusually large quantities of fuel for any purpose, he had but to declare fire *tabu*, and the common people ate their food raw, that the chief's whim might be gratified; sometimes silence was enjoined by a more than usually despotic chief, and then not only were the people forbidden to speak, but dogs were muzzled, and chickens confined in calabashes to prevent their cackling.

The penalty for breaking *tabu* was death.

But the *tabu* operated more widely against a woman — perhaps to equalize the other unusual privileges she enjoyed. There were dozens of things she might not do, the doing of which would have done naught save perhaps to give her a little comfort. With that chivalrous consideration for his womankind by which uncivilized man is distinguished all over the world, the most toothsome

HAWAIIAN-AMERICA

products of the islands were forbidden to her; nor was she permitted to eat the few varieties of her menu at the same time or in the same room with the men. Several kinds of fish (some of the most desirable), cocoanuts, bananas, pork, and turtle, were all *tabu* to women.

And all the land had passed into the absolute

HAWAIIAN CALABASHES

control of the ruling chiefs; it was a feudalism backed by a despotism that brooked no mediation. The chiefs owned all the land, the products of the soil, the fish in the sea, and the people. They gave and they took away, as suited the royal pleasure. The ruling chiefs kept such land as they desired for their immediate individual use, and divided the rest among their sub-chiefs, who again divided it among smaller chiefs, who portioned it out to the individual toilers of the various sections.

IN FEUDAL DAYS

In return the ruling chief received supplies, and, in time of war, support from the head chiefs, their sub-chiefs, and dependents. The only privilege the common people enjoyed consisted of transferring their allegiance from one great chief to another; and since from the common people was recruited the fighting force, it acted as a restraining influence upon the otherwise wanton habits of the *Alii*.

Upon the accession of a new ruling chief there was of course a complete redistribution of lands and of favors, carried to severe extremes if the change of régime came as a result of war; and if not, then the distribution was less radical, and took the form of favors to friends of the cause.

Quite a complete spoils system, in fact.

This was the political and social condition of these Hawaiian Islands when Cook paid his first visit in 1778.

Almost within a year of his landing, the relations that began on a basis so friendly had, through the thievish tendencies of the native men, the lustful searchings of the foreign sailors, and the yielding temperament of the native women, led to a mêlée, which resulted in Captain Cook's death at the hands of a native man, the bombardment of the near-by native village (Napoopoo, island of Hawaii), and the departure (February, 1779) of Cook's vessels. The story of the quarrels and of Cook's death lost nothing in the telling by the returning crews, and

HAWAIIAN-AMERICA

the Sandwich-Islanders thus early achieved a reputation for savagery which they never merited, and which subsequent events proved they did not possess.

It may be supposed that the experience with the Cook expedition did not leave a favorable impression of the white race with the natives.

WOODEN IDOL

Seven years passed before another foreign ship touched at Hawaii, and then two English vessels, *King George* and *Queen Charlotte*, commanded by Captains Portlock and Dixon, anchored in Kealakeakua Bay—where Cook had been killed, and where to-day stands a stone monument to his memory erected by the natives—but were not made welcome, and sailed to other Hawaiian islands, where they succeeded in doing some trading. The same year (1786) a French ship put in at the islands for trade, and in the succeeding two or three years ships engaged in the fur trade began to make the islands a place of call on their way to the north, and not infrequently spent the winter in one of the island ports.

There was no disturbance with the natives, until an American fur-trader, named Metcalf (in 1779),

IN FEUDAL DAYS

perpetrated a cowardly act of outrageous cruelty upon the natives—in revenge for some small dispute over a stolen boat—which resulted in the death of half a dozen canoe-loads of natives, and the capture by natives, in retaliation, of one of the two American ships, and the killing of all save two of her officers and crew. These two survivors were Isaac Davis and John Young, both of whom were kindly treated, raised to the rank of *Alii*, given

IMPLEMENTS USED IN THE MANUFACTURE OF *KAPA*

native wives, and finally were closely concerned in the civilization of the Hawaiians—Young eventually becoming Prime Minister.

We come now to the most impressive figure in Hawaiian history, Kamehameha I.—or the Great, as he is called—the only impressive native figure, indeed, that Hawaii has produced. Kamehameha was born in 1737, on the island of Hawaii, whence came the first ruling families, and wherefor the present and official name of the group. At the time of Cook's first visit Kamehameha was already a distinguished and unusually skilled commander, who had with great success entered the civil strife between chiefs, in those years convulsing the islands.

The capture of the American ship with its guns, and the possession of small-arms and ammunition received from China in trade for sandal-wood, led Kamehameha to enter upon the conquest of all the islands—a resolution formed some years before, and to which end he had waged more or less constant warfare. So, in 1790, we find him crossing over to the island of Maui with a large force of warriors, a number of whom bore fire-arms, which Young and Davis had taught them to use.

Successful in Maui, Kamehameha returned to his own island of Hawaii, where, after several months of severe fighting—for on this big island were other chiefs of valor and skill—and the loss of many men, Kamehameha's persistence, and the brave showing of his men and muskets, carried the day, and Hawaii was added to Maui, under the one great chief.

Encouraged by this success, Kamehameha set out upon the longer journey and the supposedly more hazardous work of subduing Oahu, where there were wealthy chiefs and numerous warriors. His fleet, including several small sailing-vessels and hundreds of large canoes, started on its journey of 150 miles, and, eventually landing where is

A NATIVE FISHERMAN

IN FEUDAL DAYS

now Honolulu, found and engaged the enemy in the beautiful Nuanuu Valley, defeating and finally driving them, utterly routed, up through the valley and over the precipice, or *pali*, which to-day is one of the famed sights of the islands.

It is worth noting here that in the previous year the chiefs of Oahu, after raising the English flag, had met on board the British ship *Discovery*, and formally placed the islands under the protectorate of Great Britain, but the cession was not ratified in England.

With this signal victory in 1795 the entire group may be said to have come practically under the control of Kamehameha, and the monarchy to have been virtually inaugurated. For although it was about fifteen years before Kauai finally surrendered, nevertheless, from the fall of the Oahu high chief, Kamehameha controlled island affairs, and visiting white traders really found but the one government. In 1810 official allegiance came also from Kauai.

With Kamehameha's accession to the high rulership of the islands, the fullest and severest application of the feudal land system was enforced. The first act of the conqueror was to divest the erstwhile enemies of their power—and land meant power—so there was a thorough redistribution of all the lands, and Kamehameha became at last, by virtue of his conquest and the feudal land system, the practical fountain-head of land tenures for all Hawaii.

It is not possible to view this only great (native) figure of Hawaiian history without yielding him respect and admiration. He had been a warrior from earliest youth; he had lived by war and war had made him; yet, having consolidated the islands under one governmental head, he strove by attention to agriculture to raise the people from the miserable poverty to which fighting had reduced them. Some time afterwards, when a great plague came that carried off his people in vast numbers and brought distress and famine to the land, Kamehameha not only set his soldiers at work in the fields, but turned to the soil himself, toiling all day with the more lowly.

He was progressive, brave, and generous. Beginning with clubs as weapons, and canoes as transports, he ended with guns and ships. On his return to Hawaii in 1808, to suppress a rebellion, his fleet of ships numbered about forty, ranging from twenty to forty tons burden each; and it was not long before he had secured a two-hundred-ton vessel, which he used in the sandal trade then flourishing. He built a coral fort at Honolulu, on advice of John Young, Prime Minister, mounted it with cannon, and successfully demanded the withdrawal of the Russians, who, in 1809, had landed with the idea of establishing a colony, and had erected a fort at Waimea, from which the Russian flag was flown. Finally, when Kaumualii, the ruling chief of Kauai, surrendered, in 1811, Kamehameha treated him with generosity unexampled in uncivilized warfare.

IN FEUDAL DAYS

During the fifty years in which Kamehameha the Great stood as the central figure of the Sandwich Islands he advanced from very near the lowest state of savagery to the very verge of civilization. In the latter days of his life, it is evident, his faith in idolatry was lessening, and before he died he forbade the human sacrifice, which from time immemorial had been the popular Hawaiian feature of all important occasions. During his wise and vigorous reign industrial activity began, and affairs generally settled to a degree the country had long been unaccustomed to enjoying. Undisturbed and so long possession of their land by the chiefs, and consequently by the proletariat dependent upon them, developed a sentiment favorable to the establishment of permanent individual rights. There is no doubt such a sentiment had become well defined in the mind of Kamehameha, for during the last few years of his life it was a subject of frequent discussion with his immediate advisers.

On Hawaii, the island of his birth, Kamehameha died (1819), at the age of eighty-two, showing at the last what civilization had accomplished by forbidding the sacrifice of human life—an offering to the gods, which his father had taught him would prolong his life.

Primitive Hawaii really ceased to exist in the middle of Kamehameha's reign; officially, however, the era closed with his death.

CHAPTER XV

WANE OF NATIVE RULE

HAWAIIAN political history has been brief but full of action. It begins with the death of Kamehameha the Great, in 1819, and, for our present purpose, ends with annexation to the United States in 1898 — seventy-nine years — during the course of which a people were reclaimed to Christian education from idolatrous ignorance, their islands cultivated, their homes bettered, and with practically no bloodshed.

The peaceful conquest of civilization!

When Kamehameha the Great died, the government of the islands passed practically into the care of his favorite widow, Kaahumanu, whom he had appointed *Kuhina nui* (a minister having veto on the King's acts), and who exercised great influence over Liholiho, the son succeeding to the throne as Kamehameha II. Kaahumanu was a woman of considerable force of character, and her association with Kamehameha I. had broadened her views and given her convictions especially on the questions of land tenure and *tabu*, for the

WANE OF NATIVE RULE

carrying out of which she was not lacking in courage.

When, therefore, Liholiho, on ascending the throne, proposed a redistribution of the lands, in accordance with the time-honored custom (and divisions always extended from the sea to the moun-

AN UP-TO-DATE HAWAIIAN (NATIVE) RIDING-HABIT

tain-top, in order to include water, pasture, and wood), Kaahumanu recognized retrogression from the forward movement instituted by her departed King, and opposed it vigorously. So vigorously, in fact, and with such indorsement by the united strength of the landed interests—which had become firmly vested in the chiefs during the long reign of Kamehameha I.—that Liholiho relinquished his purpose. And thus for the first time in Hawaiian history was instituted a permanent settlement of the landed interests in the kingdom, afterwards developed somewhat, in fairness to the common people of the islands, but never ignored.

Following closely upon this victory over an ancient custom, Kaahumanu induced Liholiho to break that most sacred *tabu* forbidding men and women eating together, and with it fell the entire system of *tabus*, the destruction of the idols, and the firing of the temples.

But these customs were of too long standing to be suddenly cast off without disturbance, and a rebellion immediately followed upon this iconoclastic festival, which Kaahumanu had been so largely concerned in organizing. Peace was soon established, however, through victory of the King's forces, and Hawaii then presented the unique spectacle of a people without a religion. 'Twas in this year, 1820, that the first missionaries came to the islands.

Although Liholiho's land policy had provided a certain amount of security in possession, yet the sovereign held in fact feudal authority over all the lands of the islands. There was growing a sentiment strongly favoring descent of land from par-

ent to child, and some adjustment that would include the common people in the distribution of privileges. Indeed, the people who were in reality the tenants, the tillers of the soil, had felt none of the favorable influences which had improved the status of their chiefs. They were as yet in reality serfs, with no landed interests, and only enjoyed profit from a slight proportion of the labor they gave their immediate chief in return for the privilege of working the soil.

They were not actually exchanged with the land, as part and parcel of its belongings, but they had scarcely civil rights. They leased their land from their chief, and paid a heavy rental in the way of labor for their landlord, besides being called upon for public work of various kinds. And they could be ejected from their holdings without notice and without hope of redress. This uncertainty of reaping the harvests of their own sowing led many of the common people to attach themselves to chiefs, whereby at least they made sure of being fed and housed in return for the desultory service of a hanger-on: a practice arising entirely from insecurity of land tenure, and perhaps the most detrimental to the industrial activity of the islands.

Nevertheless, feudalism was waning. The miserable and defenceless condition of the common people and the paralyzation of island industry certain to follow on their abandonment of the fields, led to much agitation of the subject among the leading natives, chiefs, and the foreigners, whose numbers were continually increasing, and finally, in 1839, to the promulgation by Kamehameha III. of his Bill of Rights—the Hawaiian Magna Charta—which although decidedly vague in defining the rights of the land it granted, yet guaranteed to the common people civil rights and protection and the right to hold property.

But the question of the proportionate interests of King, chiefs, and the common people, in the land of the islands, remained to be settled, the tenure of the people meanwhile resting on the extent of their industrial cultivation. Nor was all the difficulty over land tenure with the natives. The industrial activity following upon the Bill of Rights attracted foreign investment and led to many vexatious disputes; among others, one in 1843, with an Englishman named Charlton, which resulted in intimidation of the Hawaiian King by the British ship of war *Carrysfort*, commanded by Paulet, and the temporary cession of the islands to England. This enforced and second cession, however, the English government failed to ratify, as they had the first and voluntary one made to Captain George Vancouver — an honored name in Hawaiian history—by the chiefs of Oahu in 1794.

These difficulties with foreigners developed an opposition among Hawaiians to permitting others than natives acquiring land on the islands. For several years there was decided agitation, and Hawaii entered upon a transition period, which in 1845, '46, and '47 developed into the organization of: (1) an Executive Ministry; (2) an Executive Department; and (3) a Judiciary Department. These much-needed and comprehensive acts, detaching the responsible government from the person of the King, marked the entrance of the missionaries into Hawaiian politics; and the entrance of the missionary into Hawaiian politics first gave Hawaii assurance of an equitable, stable government.

It now became apparent that the divorce of government and King, as an accepted feature of the political system, would not be complete until the government had public lands, and was the acknowledged source of land-titles. Therefore, after the appointment of various boards and commissions, and the elaboration of laws, the great division of the lands among the King, the chiefs, and the people was finally accomplished in 1848, only nine years after the people were recognized as having any rights by Kamehameha III.

The division of the land " involved the surrender by the chiefs of a third of their estates to the government, or a payment in lieu thereof in money, as had been already required of the tenant landholders. The division between the King and the chiefs was effected through partition deeds signed by both parties; the chiefs then went before the Land Commission and received awards for the lands thus partitioned off to them, and subsequently many of them commuted for the remaining one-third interest of the government by the surrender of a portion." When the division between the King and his chiefs had been completed, the King again divided the lands that had been surrendered to him by the chiefs, between himself and the government; the lands retained by the King being known thereafter as crown lands, and those thus given to the government, as government lands.

Thus was accomplished the great land reform, that had in less than ten years delivered these people from the tyranny and serfdom of feudalism to the enjoyment of civil rights and security in landed interests. And in twenty-five years had come written language, conversion to Christianity, courts of justice, fixed and stable government, schools, and a rapidly decreasing illiteracy.

So long as the Kamehameha dynasty reigned over Hawaii, as it did, without interruption, until the death in 1872 of the fifth of that name and race, the political and industrial life of the islands thrived. The government was broadened and strengthened, public works entered upon, the school system developed, and an absolute unity of interest and harmony of action existed between the natives and the whites, more especially the American residents.

And there was excellent reason for this friendli-

A ROYAL *LUAU* AT THE KING'S BOAT-HOUSE

WANE OF NATIVE RULE

ness towards Americans, for twice (1831, 1843) had that country intervened in Hawaii's behalf with England, and once with France, not to add that the traders, the educators, the commerce and the prosperity of the islands all practically came from the United States. Therefore, a treaty between the countries was to be expected, and on December 20, 1849, it came and was ratified by the United States Senate, February 4, 1850. So far back as 1821, a sailing-ship captain, Thomas Jones, had negotiated a treaty with the United States, but Congress, with its usual wisdom—of which it has since made startling revelations on various Hawaiian occasions—declined to ratify it.

With the ratification of the treaty in 1850, a sentiment favoring annexation to the United States became apparent on the islands, and was first made publicly manifest in an effort to escape the demands of France, by the cession to the United States of the islands by Kamehameha III., ratified by both houses of the Hawaiian Parliament, June, 1851. Though this was not ratified by the Senate, the United States government advised Hawaii of its good offices, and the aggressive attitude France had maintained for several years towards Hawaii changed. Trade with the United States was increasing, and with it an obviously strong under-current of feeling in Hawaii that desired political annexation with the mainland.

The death of Kamehameha V. leaving the Hawaiian throne without either natural or appointed heir, Lunalilo, by birth the highest in the line of chiefs, was elected by popular and endorsed by legislative vote. He died a year later, without issue, and without an appointed successor, so it became the duty of the Hawaiian legislature (1874) to elect a King to the island throne.

And with this election began Hawaii's internal troubles, that ceased not until her destiny had been joined with that of the country which for half a century had stood her sponsor before the world.

For the first time in the history of the islands, the throne of Hawaii was disputed. One faction favored Emma, the Dowager Queen of Kamehameha IV., and as she was the adopted daughter of an English physician, and granddaughter of the wrecked English sailor, John Young—who taught Kamehameha the Great how to use cannon, and then settled down on Hawaii and raised a family—this faction enlisted the active support of English residents and the sympathies of English influence. The other faction supported Kalakaua, purported to be a descendant of one of the smaller chiefs of the island, but commonly reputed to be of less honorable birth.

Of the two, Emma certainly was the more creditable representative, and but for her well-known hostility to all things American, she probably would have been chosen. So Kalakaua was elected by the legislature, and a small-sized riot ensued, started by Emma's henchmen, who sacked the rooms of the executive building, assaulted some of the representatives, and were not quelled until, for the first time in the history of the island monarchy, troops were asked for from the United States war-ships *Tuscarora* and *Portsmouth:* a force of 150 landing, dispersing the mob, and restoring order. Queen Emma proved her excellent sense by accepting the decision of the legislature without question.

Although during the reign of Kalakaua commercial relations with the United States and Hawaii developed the reciprocity treaty, and the commerce of the islands went forward with a great rush, it was by no means to be attributed to the wisdom or business acumen of the King. The ascension of Kalakaua in fact marks the wane of native rule in Hawaii.

Kalakua was the first King since civilization had overtaken Hawaii to give free reign to the instincts of Polynesian savagery that stirred in him. No doubt identical feelings had at times moved his predecessors, but except for a trivial display by Kamehameha IV., the Kings had shown a desire to follow the suggestions of their white advisers— and they always had good advisers from the first landing of the missionaries.

A less suitable man than Kalakaua on the throne at this particular time of Hawaii's progression could hardly have been chosen. He was too egotistical to take advice, too self-satisfied to hearken to warning, too ignorant to appreciate that he, the representative of a weak, thriftless, dying race, held his throne by the sufferance of the stronger, civilized people that had brought prosperity to his islands.

Kalakaua was in no way related to the only royal family Hawaii ever had, the Kamehamehas, and in every way he revealed the lack of dignity and the greed for notorious extravagances commonly displayed by the man of low intellect raised to unusual prominence.

He had been a man of dissolute habits before ascending the throne, and his habits did not change for the better after he was crowned King of Hawaii. In point of fact, they changed for the worse. His associates before had been drawn from an irresponsible class with loose morals, and these now came to swell his court of dissipated dependants. The government revenues had grown large, owing to the profit in sugar-making — and what were government revenues for, but to give the King and his cronies a good time? What concern had a King whose dearest wish was to be considered a prince of good fellows for public works, educational systems, charitable institutions?

So Kalakaua and his crew of parasites drank and feasted and gambled, while yet the patience of the white people and the better class of natives lasted.

The King was superstitious, corrupt, and sensual; he believed in sorcery, and made an effort to give

WANE OF NATIVE RULE

the *kahunas* official recognition, going so far as to organize a government board of health, which was to be composed of these relics of a savage faith. His financial intrigues were as notorious as corrupt: bribery from Chinamen for opium license being accepted, and towards the last days of the monarchy, it is said, the Chinese and Japanese were

THE KING'S BOAT-HOUSE, WHERE THE CARES OF STATE WERE DISSIPATED IN KALAKAU'S REIGN

paying for verdicts in the lower courts; added to these were the revolting sprees, in which lustful desires and lewd performances were the features, and the King a prominent performer.

Debauchery ruled in private life, and bribery and extravagance and pernicious legislation in the government.

In 1879 the King's appointment as Minister of Foreign Affairs of an Italian adventurer, Moreno, with wild schemes and ultra jingo ideas, resulted in the first white interference with native rule. A mass-meeting of citizens demanded the dismissal of the Moreno cabinet, and was sustained in its position by the diplomatic representatives of foreign governments. Though the King yielded (reluctantly), yet did he fail to recognize the implied warning against the future.

Having made one trip to the United States (1874) and another around the world (1881), and celebrated the fiftieth anniversary of his birth with great extravagance and long feasting (at public cost), Kalakaua conceived the idea of uniting all Southern Pacific interests and crowning himself Emperor of Polynesia. In pursuance of his ambition, a ship was purchased, fitted out at considerable expense as a man-of-war, and under command of one of the King's assortment of human tanks, despatched to Apia to assume a protectorate over the Samoan Islands, another one of the King's revellers being sent as envoy to King Malietoa. The expedition resulted as only could be expected. The envoy entered upon a debauch that brought him disgrace, and the captain of the ship sold his ammunition and guns for gin; bombastic notices sent to all foreign powers were the only tangible results of Kalakaua's great scheme for Pacific supremacy.

EVENTIDE

WANE OF NATIVE RULE

The Hawaiian King was speedily to have other surprises more shocking.

There came finally a day when the patience of the white citizens and that of the best class of natives and half-whites was exhausted by the continued extravagance and disgraceful corruption and shameless debauchery of Kalakaua. On June 30, 1887, it found expression in a mass-meeting which voted disapproval of the administration of the Hawaiian government and lack of confidence in the future under existing methods, and appointed a committee to wait on the King.

This committee, with the moral support of all foreign diplomatic representatives, demanded within twenty-four hours assurance of future honest, progressive government on the basis of a new constitution, and Kalakaua, craven-hearted sot that he was, and fearful lest he lose his crown, agreed to all the demands of the citizens. Quite a proportion of the meeting wished for the abolition of the monarchy, but deliberate discussion of the matter showed the general sense of the meeting to be not radical change, if possible to avoid it, not injury to the King, but improvement that would give assurance of future honesty and progression.

The new constitution exacted from Kalakaua, among other things decidedly bettered the status of citizenship, giving every man of American or European descent, who took the oath of allegiance, the legal right to vote after one year's residence in the islands. It took from the King his right of absolute veto, and placed the responsibility of government upon a cabinet appointed by the King, but subject to change only by the vote of a legislature elected by the people. It prescribed an income of certain amount necessary to all voters; and this gave the white residents—who were contributing about ninety per cent. of the public revenues—some voice in its disbursement. It forbade members of the legislature to hold civil office. In a word, it gave suffrage to the white residents, in whom all Hawaii's commercial interests were vested, and held out the future promise of public money being used for public improvement, so sorely needed, and which Kalakaua's control of the legislature before the enfranchisement of the whites had made impossible.

But such a radical change was not to come about without difficulty. The adventurers and the parasites that had hung about the King's person were not to lose their easy living without a struggle, and numerous revolutionary plots were put together, only to fall to pieces without maturing, because of the weakness of their sponsors. There was one discontented spirit, however, R. W. Wilcox, a half-white whom Kalakaua had sent to Italy under Moreno for education at government expense, who planned more persistently and was said to be backed by Princess Liliuokalani, sister of the King and heiress apparent, who had bitterly upbraided her brother upon his acceding to the reform constitution.

Together Wilcox and Liliuokalani planned the paltry revolt that on July 31, 1889, made demonstration in the palace yard, with the idea of restoring the old corrupt government. Wilcox's forces consisted of all the malcontents and loafers of Honolulu, but the same men who had exacted good government from Kalakaua reorganized, and speedily dispersed Wilcox and his gang, killing nine of them and making prisoners of the remainder. Although the native vote subsequently put Wilcox and several of his aides in the legislature, and there were attempts to amend the constitution wrested from Kalakaua, yet the spirit of the reform party prevailed, and their work stood as the law of the kingdom.

Prosperity came to the islands, public works were erected, needed roads made, docks constructed— and January 20, 1891, Kalakaua died in the Palace Hotel, San Francisco, whither he had gone seeking recuperation from his Honolulu debaucheries.

CHAPTER XVI

FALL OF THE MONARCHY

HAD Liliuokalani kept the oath (to maintain the constitution) she took on accession to the Hawaiian throne, January 29, 1891, there can be little doubt that she would now be reigning, and the islands an independent kingdom under the *quasi* protection of a great and generous power—the United States. Her reign began with the best wishes of all the white residents, who earnestly hoped for a cessation of the political intrigue and corruption which had characterized Kalakaua's reign, and stood ready to support her warmly in every act for the peace and prosperity of the islands.

It must be as frankly stated, however, that although the Queen inspired more confidence than had her deceased brother, whom she succeeded, nevertheless that confidence was not an abiding one, either among the white residents, who knew the Queen's hostility towards them, or among a considerable class of natives, who had remained faithful to Queen Emma.

Liliuokalani's assumption of the crown may in

truth be said to have been viewed with anxiety by all foreign residents. She had given some indications of an obstinate will, while representing her brother during the latter's trip around the world; and her bitter opposition to the new constitution exacted from Kalakaua, and her implacable resentment of white suffrage, were quite sufficient to create apprehension for the future. Many believed, and with good reason, that she would not take the oath, and when she did, the sincerity of the act was doubted.

As in her brother, the Polynesian instincts were predominant; in Kalakaua they had been gratified in basest debauchery and extravagant living; in Liliuokalani they were disclosed in persistent promotion of race prejudice, and in harboring pagan superstitions, and in the violence of spirit against civilized procedure. Each in quality of intellect and in character of heart was much inferior to any of Hawaii's previous sovereigns. In both the savage was ascendant: weak and vacillating and vicious in the brother; courageous and obstinate and cruel in the sister. Had they followed the example of their predecessors and been guided by the wisdom of white advisers, their reigns no doubt would have been equally happy, but instead they ignored precedent, and it was fitting that, entirely because of their own acts, their reigns should mark, first, the wane of native rule, and, finally, the fall of the monarchy.

Queen Liliuokalani gave evidence at the very outset that her reign was to be a determined effort for a return to absolutism. On accession she successfully demanded the resignation of the cabinet, being sustained by the supreme court—which, in the absence of any precedent and of any definite law touching the subject, declared the cabinet positions to have been vacated at the King's death—and forthwith proceeded to name a cabinet pliant to her wishes and of well-known inimicality to foreign interests. The legislature, however, failed to sustain her action, and forthwith a struggle for supremacy between Queen and legislature was inaugurated. Three of the Queen's cabinets were voted out one after the other in rapid succession, lists of candidates presented and rejected, until at length, evidently convinced of her inability to secure her desires in that manner, Liliuokalani submitted an acceptable cabinet which became known as the Wilcox-Jones ministry.

But this was only postponing the inevitable crisis. The Queen was determined to create a new constitution in sympathy with her anti-foreign sentiments, and it was not long, in fact, before her intentions to that end were proclaimed on the streets by her enthusiastic though unwise supporters.

At the time Liliuokalani made up her Wilcox-Jones cabinet, very wealthy and unscrupulous agents of a lottery company and of an opium ring were seeking foothold in Hawaii, much against the

wishes of the people. Immediately entering into conspiracy with these, the Queen agreed to grant the required lottery franchise and opium license in return for help in overturning the legislature. The scheme went forward, adroitly though rascally managed. Alluring bribes were given by the opium ring to "approachable" native legislators, and lottery stock issued to conspirators both in and out of the legislature.

The respectable members of the legislature used their utmost endeavors to hold the body aloof from corruption; the best element in Honolulu appealed to the Queen for relief from the impending crisis, but to no avail. The legislature was polluted, the bills passed, and the Queen, January 14, 1893, announced her intention of abrogating the constitution of 1887 she had taken oath to uphold, and promulgating a new one embodying her well-known views.

Among other things, Liliuokalani's new constitution denied suffrage to all white men not married to native women, and provided that members of the Senate and of the State Council should not be elected, but appointed at will by the Queen.

The effect of the Queen's attitude was, of course, to paralyze all business and set Honolulu agog with excitement. The cabinet sought to dissuade the Queen from her proposed action, telling her it was a revolutionary act, assuring her it would cause bloodshed; but for reply Liliuokalani threatened her ministers with punishment if they did not unite with her in proclaiming the new constitution.

Meantime, with excitement running high, a public mass-meeting was held and a "Committee of Public Safety" appointed, which comprised Henry Waterhouse, W. C. Wilder, Lorrin A. Thurston, William O. Smith, Theodore F. Lansing, C. Bolte, John Emmeluth, Andrew Brown, J. A. McCandless, Edward Suhr, F. W. McChesney, and Henry E. Cooper, chairman. Two days later the citizens of Honolulu held another mass-meeting, which adopted resolutions condemning the action of the Queen and authorizing the Committee of Safety to "further devise such ways and means as may be necessary to secure the permanent maintenance of law, order, and the protection of life, liberty, and property in Hawaii."

Meantime the Queen, who had abandoned the palace and retired to her residence with her followers, posted a proclamation in Hawaiian to her native subjects, promising a constitution which would please them. The town was now in a condition bordering on terrorism, fires started in various quarters of the city, the women and the less brave among the men were panic-stricken, and in this extremity the Committee of Safety appealed to the United States Minister, Honorable John L. Stevens, for the protection of the town from riot and possible loss of life. Mr. Stevens requested Captain G. C. Wiltse, commanding the *Boston*, then in the

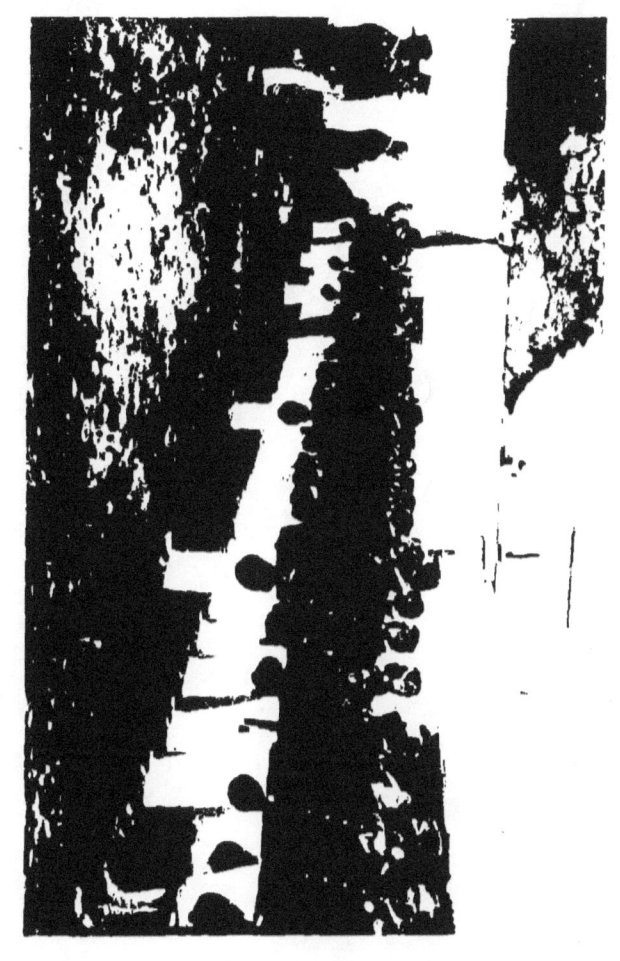

TAKING THE OATH OF ALLEGIANCE TO THE UNITED STATES—THE HAWAIIAN POLICE FORCE BEING SWORN IN AFTER THE FLAG-RAISING CEREMONIES

FALL OF THE MONARCHY

harbor, to land a force of marines and sailors for the protection of the United States Legation, and to guard the safety of American citizens and their property. The force landed in three squads; two guarded the Legation and Consulate, and the third quartered in Arion Hall, near the centre of the town. Especial care was taken that the landing and disposition of the squads be accomplished with no ostentation that could be misconstrued as partisan, and the men were kept entirely out of sight at their respective quarters.

Their presence, however, undoubtedly saved Honolulu from incendiarism and riot that night.

On the next day, January 17th, before a large mass-meeting, the Committee of Public Safety deposed Liliuokalani—who by her declared and published intention to abrogate the constitution she had sworn to uphold had virtually abdicated her sovereignty—and organized a provisional government, "to exist until terms of union with the United States of America have been negotiated and agreed upon." The Queen acquiesced under protest; the representatives of all the foreign governments recognized the Provisional Government.

And thus fell the monarchy.

Sanford B. Dole, Associate Justice of the Supreme Court, was elected President of the new government, with a strong advisory council, and immediate steps were taken to maintain their integrity at home and to spare them from complications abroad. Two days after the abrogation of the monarchy, the Provisional Government chartered a steamer and sent a commission, composed of Lorrin A. Thurston, W. C. Wilder, Joseph Marsden, Charles L. Carter, and William R. Castle, to Washington *via* San Francisco, to negotiate a treaty of annexation to the United States.

Meantime, for fear that the Japanese or other power might take advantage of the unsettled situation and seek a joint protectorate over the islands, the Provisional Government very sensibly asked Minister Stevens to establish a temporary American protectorate pending results at Washington, to which Mr. Stevens consented by hoisting the American flag over the executive building at Honolulu.

At Washington negotiations had proceeded happily, a treaty was drawn and signed, by the terms of which the United States assumed the islands' public debt and became the owners of all the public lands and other public property of the Hawaiian Islands. It was further agreed that Liliuokalani should receive an annual pension of $20,000 (about one-quarter of her income as Queen), and the late Princess Kaiulani (who as heir-apparent received $5000 a year) was to be given a lump sum of $150,000. This money to be given, of course, conditional on their peaceful acquiescence in the annexation.

On February 17, 1893, President Harrison sent

the treaty to the United States Senate, with a full discussion of the case and his complete indorsement of the conclusion.

And the prospects for Hawaii were roseate.

On March 3, 1893, Congress adjourned without action on the treaty, and the following day Grover Cleveland was inaugurated President of the United States.

CHAPTER XVII

BIRTH OF THE REPUBLIC—AND ANNEXATION

GROVER CLEVELAND'S endeavors as President of the United States to restore the corrupt and semi-barbaric Hawaiian monarchy will always remain a disappointment to his friends in and out of his particular party. Not only that his course must, from a purely unprejudiced standpoint, be viewed as a gross political blunder, singularly unmindful of the popular sentiment in America, but because it revealed antagonism which denied even common fairness to the subject of his displeasure, and showed a purpose so set in the accomplishment of its desires, as to countenance intrigue utterly undignified in the Chief Executive of this or any other country.

Mr. Cleveland's attitude on the Hawaiian question, in fine, was so violently prejudiced as to barely escape censure from the special Senate Committee on Foreign Affairs, which cleared the Honorable John L. Stevens and Captain Wiltze of the charges (connivance with the Provisional Government in the abrogation of the monarchy) made by "Paramount" Blount and indorsed by his sponsor, Grover Cleveland.

It was a "policy of infamy," that began by discrediting the full and unbiassed investigation which had preceded Benjamin Harrison's signing of the annexation treaty, was continued by the (directed) efforts of Minister Willis to secretly and diligently plot for the overthrow of the Provisional Government to which he was accredited, and closed by the deliberate withdrawal from Honolulu, against the earnest protest of its commander, of the only United States war-ship there—an action that gave the hint to the ex-Queen's followers and resulted in their uprising and several days of fighting. But for the vigilance of the Provisional Government this revolt would have been a night massacre.

It will be many years before the odium attaching to the names of Cleveland, Blount, and Willis for their connection with the Hawaiian "question" will be removed.

President Cleveland withdrew from the United States Senate the annexation treaty which had been signed by his predecessor, Benjamin Harrison, entirely because of the disparity between President Harrison's official comment, that "the overthrow of the monarchy was not in any way promoted by this government," and Cleveland's professed belief that "the lawful government of Hawaii [the monarchy] was overthrown . . . by a process every step of which . . . is directly traceable to and dependent for its safety upon the agency of the United States acting through its diplomatic [John L. Stevens] and naval [Captain Wiltze] representatives." Subsequently, after special investigation, the Senate Committee on For-

DETACHMENT OF AMERICAN MARINES ENTERING THE EXECUTIVE GROUNDS AT HONOLULU WITH THE OFFICIAL FLAG TO BE HOISTED OVER THE GOVERNMENT BUILDING

eign Affairs, which included Senator Morgan (of the same party affiliations as President Cleveland), published an official opinion contrary to that of Cleveland's (based on the prejudice and *ex-*

parte investigations of "Paramount" Blount) and vindicated both John L. Stevens and Captain Wiltze.

President Cleveland withdrew the annexation treaty from the consideration of the Senate on the fifth day after his inauguration, and on March 11, 1893, appointed James H. Blount, of Georgia, as his special commissioner to Hawaii.

Though somewhat surprising in its implied discrediting of all the investigation already made, Hawaiians at first saw in this merely an extreme conservative desire for further inquiry, and were prepared to give the President's commissioner every possible assistance. Mr. Blount inaugurated his arrival at Honolulu by discourtesy to the Provisional Government delegation which received him, and revealed his sympathies by taking up residence in the midst of the ex-Queen's most loyal supporters. Still there would not necessarily have been any indication of bias in this had the other side received equal consideration.

From the very day Mr. Blount landed, and through all the days of his sojourn until he departed, August 8, 1893, he gave unmistakable evidence of his sympathies and of the nature of the report he was certain to make. He dwelt in the midst of the friends of the monarchy—the royalists, so called—listened to all they had to say, noted their evidence, accepted their social attentions. To the other side he was scarcely civil, declining their invitations and viewing their evidence with obvious suspicion.

It became evident before Mr. Blount had been in the islands a month, that he was not a commissioner seeking the true facts of the local situation, but rather an agent bent on securing all possible evidence to support further effort for the restoration of the monarchy. And in this impression he was ably seconded by a sensation-seeking newspaper reporter, who, indifferent to facts, appeared to be his mouth-piece, and by Claus Spreckels, who urged the planters to support the royalists because it guaranteed coolie labor, and, failing to enlist their coöperation, denounced them. It was an *ex-parte* investigation from beginning to end, and Blount's report, filled with untruth, was rightfully denounced by the Senate Committee.

Having gathered his *ex-parte* data, and encouraged the royalists, Blount returned to the United States, and about three months later (November 4, 1893) the new American Minister, Albert Willis, arrived at Honolulu. Meantime a damaging state of unrest prevailed in both the business and social circles of the islands. The Queen's followers, being for the most part the undesirable elements of the town, assumed a tone of confident swagger, and capital and industry shrunk under the possibility of a restored monarchy, with the well-known extreme and anti-foreign views of Liliuokalani prevailing.

Mr. Willis came to Honolulu, accredited to the Provisional Government, and with a friendly letter to its President, Sanford Dole, from President Cleveland, beginning, "My great and good Friend," and Mr. Willis remained to plot, under the instructions of President Cleveland, with the relics of a corrupt monarchy against the government to which he was accredited! Modern history contains no more extraordinary incident. The Chief Executive of an enlightened, progressive, democratic country entering into a covert alliance to restore a semi-barbaric, wholly corrupt Queen over a kingdom that owed its civilization, education, prosperity to the white people, whose interests amounted to ninety per cent. of the islands' wealth, and whose will had deposed the Queen!

One week after his arrival, Mr. Willis secretly sent for Liliuokalani, and, informing her that she had been deposed through the "reprehensible conduct of the American Minister," and the "unauthorized presence on land of a military force of the United States," said that President Cleveland intended restoring her to the throne, if she grant amnesty to all "who participated in the movement against her," and agreed to assume all obligations created by the Provisional Government in due course of administration.

Liliuokalani insisted that all who had participated in the movement must be beheaded and their property confiscated. It was not until December 18th, and after other meetings and much pressure brought upon the ex-Queen by her few remaining friends of judgment, that she agreed to grant full amnesty in case she were restored.

Meantime Minister Willis had sent reports to President Cleveland, and Secretary Gresham's note to the President, advising restoration of the monarchy, had been published, and Honolulu was in a turmoil of excitement. The plotting of Willis with the ex-Queen, which had become known to the Provisional Government through private sources, and the Gresham letter, led to a mass-meeting, November 25, 1893, at Honolulu, which protested against assumption by President Cleveland of any control over Hawaiian internal affairs, against the restoration of Liliuokalani to the Hawaiian throne, and pledged "support to the best of our ability to the Provisional Government in resisting any attacks upon it which may be contrary to the usage of nations."

On the following day President Dole demanded of Minister Willis his intention towards Hawaii, to which the latter, December 2d, sent an evasive reply. Meanwhile, Willis continued plotting with Liliuokalani, and on her agreeing to grant full amnesty, as requested at the first interview, Willis, December 19, 1893, demanded of President Dole, "in the name and by the authority of the United States of America," that he "promptly relinquish"

LANDING OF U. S. MARINES FROM THE U. S. WAR-SHIPS *PHILADELPHIA* AND *MOHICAN* FOR THE FLAG-RAISING CEREMONIES ON AUGUST 12TH

the government to Liliuokalani. In a reply that ably and impartially reviewed the causes leading to the revolution which ended in the abrogation of the monarchy, and of the political situation of the islands, and of the questions pending, President Dole respectfully and firmly refused to accede to the demand of Minister Willis, made in the name of the United States.

The situation in Honolulu following this correspondence bordered on terrorism, and may best be described by the following excerpt from a letter President Dole sent Minister Willis, December 27, 1893, earnestly seeking some conclusion of the unrest:

> ... "The enemies of the government, believing in your intentions to restore the monarchy by force, have become emboldened. Threats of assassination of the officers of this government have been made. The police force is frequently informed of conspiracies to create disorder. Aged and sick persons of all nationalities have been and are in a state of distress and anxiety. Children in the schools are agitated by the fear of political disturbances. The wives, sisters, and daughters of residents, including many Americans, have been in daily apprehension of civic disorder, many of them having even armed themselves in preparation thereof. Citizens have made preparations in their homes for defence against assaults which may arise directly or indirectly from such conflict. Persons have begun to pack their valuables with a view of immediate departure. Large quantities of bandages have been prepared. Unprotected women have received the promise of asylum from the Japanese representative, against possible disturb-

ance arising in consequence of American invasion. Rumors of the intended landing of your forces for offensive purposes have agitated the community for many days. The situation for weeks has been one of actual warfare, without the incident of actual combat. Even the ex-Queen has called upon this provisional government for protection, which has been awarded her. Owing to your attitude, the government has been compelled by public apprehension to largely increase the military force at great expense. Its offices have been placed, and still continue, in a condition of defence and preparation for a siege, and the community has been put into a state of mind bordering on terrorism."

President Cleveland had gone to the very limit of his power in his endeavor to restore the Hawaiian monarchy, and Sanford Dole's firm refusal to the demand of Willis was an issue unexpected by Cleveland and Gresham.

The President could not use the military or naval forces of the United States to establish Liliuokalani on her throne, without the authority of Congress. Therefore, Cleveland was compelled to refer the Hawaiian question in its entirety to Congress, both houses of which had already severely criticised his restoration policy. And as the intriguing and the injustice and the *ex-parte* procedure of that "policy of infamy" were disclosed, all the country joined in its condemnation.

By the middle of January, 1894, Honolulu knew the trend of public opinion in the United States on Cleveland's policy, and knew they need have no fear of Liliuokalani's restoration. In another three months it became apparent that annexation was not likely to result until a change of administration; therefore, in the hope of eventual annexation, a Republic was proclaimed, July 4, 1894, with Sanford B. Dole as President, and promptly recognized by all the foreign governments.

The constitution adopted partook of the best features of that of the United States and of the individual States. The legislature was composed of a Senate and a House of Representatives, each having fifteen members. To insure the political life of the islands against control by the ignorant and irresponsible, an educational qualification was required of voters for Representatives, and, in addition, a property qualification of those eligible to vote for the Senators. At the first election called by the Republic for Senators and Representatives, about 5000 voters qualified, and all the members of both houses were elected on a platform favoring annexation. Both houses subsequently passed resolutions approving annexation. As the majority of the members of the House of Representatives, including the Speaker, were full-blooded natives, this is suggestive of the best sentiment in Hawaii and worth remembering.

The establishment of permanent government was the signal for general industrial activity and brought peace for the present and confidence in the future. Many needed improvements were begun, and the first legislature of the Republic, which convened

June 12, 1895, provided for a division of the crown and government lands into homesteads.

But the new Republic was not to begin life at its ease. There continued much secret work by the disgruntled royalists, which resulted in a delegation waiting upon Secretary of State Gresham, and, among other things, suggesting that the royalists could reassert themselves were the United States to withdraw its war-ship from Honolulu. Whether or not in compliance with this request I do not pretend to say, but it is a fact that Admiral Walker, commanding the *Philadelphia*, then at Honolulu, received telegraphic orders July 9th to proceed to the Pacific coast. Well knowing what a pacifier his presence was in case of an island crisis, and petitioned by the leading people of the town to remain, the Admiral delayed sailing from day to day, until August 12th, when a second telegraphic order instructed him to get under way at once.

So he sailed, leaving the royalists elated and a British war-ship in the harbor. It was the first time in twenty years Hawaiian waters had been without an American war-ship.

The expected came in due course after the withdrawal of the *Philadelphia*, for on January 7, 1895, a plot was discovered which included the overthrow of the Republic and the slaughter of the government officials and their families. The insurgents were promptly met, and, after a few days' desultory firing, captured, together with arms and ammuni-

THE FLAG-RAISING CEREMONY, FRIDAY, AUGUST 12, 1898—MINISTER SEWALL PRESENTS NEWLANDS RESOLUTION TO PRESIDENT DOLE

tion, and a new constitution concealed in the ex-Queen's residence. The only loss to the Republic force was the death of Charles L. Carter, a prominent young attorney who had been one of the Washington Annexation Commission in 1893.

This was the dying effort of the royalists; the ex-Queen voluntarily, and no doubt with the hope of escaping the punishment she merited, took the oath of allegiance to the Republic, and though she was tried and sentenced to imprisonment and to pay a fine, she and all the others were eventually released and pardoned — a magnanimous conclusion of a splendid work.

With the suppression of this last attempt to overthrow the Republic, set in Hawaii's most prosperous years; public works were begun, the industries took new life, and the country thrived as it had not before, the government constantly winning native support.

The return of the Republican party to power in the election of President McKinley brought annexation at once under consideration, and a new treaty was drawn on very much the same lines as that of 1893, except for the omission of the provisions in the earlier one for pensions to Liliuokalani and Princess Kaiulani. This treaty was signed by President McKinley and sent to Congress June 16, 1897, then convened in special session, but the Senate adjourned without action. In the regular session, December 6, 1897, the Hawaiian question again came up and was discussed behind closed doors at different times during several months, without the necessary two-thirds affirmative vote being available, and therefore no vote was taken.

This was the situation when hostilities began between the United States and Spain. On May 1, 1898, Admiral Dewey achieved his brilliant naval victory before Manila, and the necessity for reinforcing him with troops and ships disclosed the need of Hawaii as a half-way refreshment station.

But Congress was not to see the light clearly, even though time was pressing and the case urgent; through two months it labored, with joint resolutions and debate, until July 6th, when the Senate declared for annexation by a vote of 42 to 21.

President McKinley signed the Annexation Joint Resolution July 7th, and on August 12, 1898, President Dole formally ceded at Honolulu the jurisdiction and property of the Republic of Hawaii to that greater Republic of the United States.

And thus the work begun so many years before came to a fitting end.

STATISTICAL

IMPORTANT EVENTS IN HAWAII'S INDUSTRIAL AND POLITICAL DEVELOPMENT

Discovery of Hawaiian Islands by Juan Gaetano (about)...............................	1555
Rediscovery by Captain James Cook..........	1778
Visit of Captain George Vancouver and introduction of first cattle and sheep.............	1792
Conquest of Islands by Kamehameha the Great and establishment of single government for the group...............................	1796
Introduction of first horse...................	1803
Death of Kamehameha the Great.............	1819
Downfall of *Tabu* system....................	1819
First Missionaries arrived on the ship *Thaddeus*	1820
Printing established.......................	1822
First commercial house established...........	1826
Treaty made with Captain T. C. Jones, U. S. S. *Peacock*—first treaty executed with any foreign power..............................	1826
First newspaper appeared...................	1836
Hawaiian Magna Charta....................	1839
Independence of Hawaii recognized by the United States............................	1842
First permanent newspaper established........	1843
Postal service established	1850
Reservoir built—Honolulu..................	1850
Treaty with United States ratified (February 4)	1850
First bank opened—Honolulu	1858

HAWAIIAN-AMERICA

Important Events (*Continued*).
 Inter-island steamboat service established—
  steamer *Kilauea*.......................... 1860
 Steam communication with the United States
  established 1866
 Reciprocity treaty with the United States...... 1875
 First island railroad—Kahului to Wailuku
  (Maui)..................................... 1879
 Marine railway built—Honolulu.............. 1883
 Cession of Pearl Harbor to United States...... 1887
 New constitution granting foreigners suffrage .. 1887
 Wilcox-Boyd riot (so-called insurrection, and
  supposed to have been incited by Liliuokalani) 1889
 Liliuokalani announced her intention to abrogate
  the constitution under which she had been
  sworn in as Queen..............January 14, 1893
 Liliuokalani deposed..............January 17, 1893
 Provisional Government established, January 17, 1893
 Formal demand on Provisional Government by
  President Grover Cleveland that Liliuokalani
  be restored to the throne.......December 19, 1893
 Republic of Hawaii proclaimed ....July 4, 1894
 Revolt of ex-Queen's adherents........January, 1895
 Annexation to United States........August 12, 1898

DISTANCES

INTER-ISLAND DISTANCES

HONOLULU TO

	Miles		Miles
Leper Settlement.........	50	Punaluu, Hawaii	250
Lahaina, Maui...........	72	Hilo, " (direct)	129
Hana, "	125	Nawiliwili, Kauai........	98
Maalaea, "	85	Waimea "	120
Mahukona, Hawaii.......	134	Hanalei, "	125
Kawaihae, "	144	Niihau	144
S. W. pt. "	233		

WIDTH OF CHANNELS
EXTREME POINT TO POINT

	Miles		Miles
Oahu and Molokai	23	Maui and Lanai	8
Diamond Head to S. W. point of Molokai	30	Maui and Kahoolawe	6
		Hawaii and Maui	26
Molokai and Lanai	8	Kauai and Oahu	61
Molokai	8	Niihau and Kauai	15

OCEAN DISTANCES
HONOLULU TO

	Miles		Miles
San Francisco	2090	Valparaiso	5916
Portland, Oregon	2460	Sydney	4480
Sitka	2395	Hong-Kong	4893
Panama	4620	Guam	3500
Tahiti	2380	Manila	4700
Samoa	2290	Yokohama	3445
Fiji	2735	Vancouver, B. C.	2330
Auckland	3850	Ocean Island	1250
Nicaragua	4210		

AREA, ELEVATION, AND POPULATION

	Area sq. miles	Acres	Highest elevation	Population 1896
Hawaii	4,210	2,000,000	13,800	33,285
Maui	760	400,000	10,032	17,726
Oahu	600	360,000	4,030	40,205
Kauai	590	350,000	4,800	15,228
Molokai	270	200,000	3,000	2,307
Lanai	150	100,000	3,000	105
Niihau	97	70,000	800	164
Kahoolawe	63	30,000	1,450	—

HAWAIIAN-AMERICA

POPULATION

TOTAL POPULATION OF ISLANDS BY CENSUS OF 1896

NATIONALITIES	Male	Female	Totals
Hawaiians	16,399	14,620	31,019
Part Hawaiians	4,249	4,236	8,485
Americans	1,975	1,111	3,086
British	1,406	844	2,250
Germans	866	566	1,432
French	56	45	101
Norwegian	216	162	378
Portuguese	8,202	6,989	15,191
Japanese	19,212	5,195	24,407
Chinese	19,167	2,449	21,616
South Sea Islanders	321	134	455
Other nationalities	448	152	600
Totals	72,517	36,503	109,020

FOREIGN BORN ON ISLANDS

NATIONALITIES	Census 1896	Census 1890	Gain	Loss
American	2,266	1,928	338	—
British	1,538	1,344	194	—
German	1,034	912	—	122
French	75	70	5	—
Portuguese	8,232	8,602	—	370
Norwegian	216	227	—	11
Japanese	22,329	17,939	4,390	—
Chinese	19,382	15,301	2,081	—

The foreign-born population has increased since last census (1890) from 41,873 to 55,783, an advance of 13,910, or 33.2 per cent.

ESTIMATED POPULATION, JANUARY 1, 1898

	Natives	Chinese	Japanese	Portuguese	All other Foreig'rs	Total
Population as per census, September, 1896	39,504	21,616	24,407	15,191	8,302	109,020
Passenger arrivals. Excess over departures, 4th quarter, 1896	—	1,377	1,673	—	339	3,389
Excess over departures for the year 1897	—	2,867	1,202	*108	695	4,872
Total	39,504	25,860	27,282	15,299	9,336	117,281

* Less 3, excess of departures in 1896.

POPULATION OF SEX, BY NATIONALITY

NATIONALITIES	HAWAIIAN BORN OF FOREIGN PARENTS			WHOLE POPULATION		
	Males	Females	Total	Males	Females	Total
Hawaiians........	--	--	—	16,399	14,620	31,019
Part Hawaiians...	—	—	—	4,249	4,236	8,485
Americans........	401	419	820	1,975	1,111	3,086
British..........	352	360	712	1,406	844	2,250
German..........	252	268	520	866	566	1,432
French..........	10	16	26	56	45	101
Norwegian	71	91	162	216	162	378
Portuguese	3,606	3,353	6,959	8,202	6,989	15,191
Japanese.........	1,054	1,024	2,078	19,212	5,195	24,407
Chinese..........	1,204	1,030	2,234	19,167	2,449	21,616
South Sea Islanders	21	25	46	321	134	455
Other nationalities.	87	89	176	448	152	600
Totals	7,058	6,675	13,733	72,517	36,503	109,020

COMPARATIVE TABLE OF NATIONALITY OF POPULATION AT VARIOUS CENSUS PERIODS SINCE 1853

NATIONALITY	1853	1866*	1872	1878	1884	1890	1896
Natives............	70,036	57,125	49,044	44,088	40,014	34,436	31,019
Part Hawaiians....	983	1,640	1,487	3,420	4,218	6,186	8,485
Chinese	364	1,206	1,938	5,916	17,937	15,301	19,382
Americans.........	692		889	1,276	2,066	1,928	2,266
Haw'n-born f'gn'rs.	309		849	947	2,040	7,495	13,733
British............	435		619	883	1,282	1,344	1,538
Portuguese	86		395	436	9,377	8,602	8,232
Germans	81	2,988	224	272	1,600	1,434	912
French............	60		88	81	192	70	75
Japanese..........	—		—	—	116	12,360	22,329
Norwegian........	8		—	—	362	227	216
Other foreigners...	80		364	666	416	419	424
Polynesian	4		—	—	956	588	409
Totals..........	73,138	62,959	56,897	57,985	80,578	89,990	109,020

* There was no complete division of nationalities noted in the census of 1866.

HAWAIIAN-AMERICA

COMPARATIVE TABLE OF POPULATION, 1836-96

ISLANDS	Census 1836	Census 1853	Census 1860	Census 1866	Census 1872	Census 1878	Census 1884	Census 1890	Census 1896
Hawaii...	39,364	24,450	21,481	19,808	16,001	17,034	24,991	26,754	33,285
Maui.....	24,199	17,574	16,400	14,035	12,334	12,109	15,970	17,357	17,726
Oahu.....	27,809	19,126	21,275	19,799	20,671	20,236	28,068	31,194	40,205
Kauai....	8,934	6,991	6,487	6,299	4,961	5,634	*8,935	11,643	15,228
Molokai..	6,000	3,607	2,864	2,299	2,349	2,581	2,614	2,652	2,307
Lanai.....	1,200	600	646	394	348	214		174	105
Niihau....	993	790	647	325	233	177	—	216	164
Kahool'we	80	—	—	—	—	—	—		
Totals..	108,579	73,138	69,800	62,959	56,897	57,985	80,578	89,990	109,020
All foreigners.....		2,119	2,716	4,194	5,366	10,477	36,346	49,368	69,516
Hawaiians........		71,019	67,084	58,765	51,531	47,508	44,232	40,622	39,504

* Including Niihau.

From Report of General Superintendent of Census

Percentage of Hawaiian-Born Foreigners

Of the total American population............ 26.5
Of the total British population 31.6
Of the total German population............. 36.3
Of the total Portuguese population........... 45.8
Of the total French population 25.7
Of the total Norwegian population........... 42.8
Of the total South Sea Islander population.... 10.1
Of the total Japanese population 8.5
Of the total Chinese population ,............ 10.3
Of the total of other nationalities............ 29.3
Of all foreign nationalities together.......... 19.7

POPULATION

PERCENTAGE OF POPULATION MARRIED AND UNMARRIED

NATIONALITIES	Number Over 15 Years	Number of Married	Per cent. Married	Per cent. Unmarried	Total Per cent.
Hawaiian males	11,250	7,150	63.56	36.44	100
Hawaiian females	9,778	8,215	84.02	15.98	100
Part-Hawaiian males	1,731	895	51.70	48.30	100
Part-Hawaiian females	1,727	1,120	64.85	35.15	100
Hawaiian-born-foreign males	445	135	30.34	69.66	100
Hawaiian-born-foreign females	444	199	44.82	55.18	100
American males	1,473	704	47.79	52.21	100
American females	592	421	71.11	28.89	100
British males	1,908	491	48.71	51.29	100
British females	436	357	81.88	18.12	100
German males	579	310	53.54	46.46	100
German females	258	212	82.17	17.83	100
French males	46	22	47.83	52.17	100
French females	28	8	28.57	71.43	100
Norwegian males	138	78	56.52	43.48	100
Norwegian females	65	54	83.08	16.92	100
Portuguese males	4,596	3,284	71.45	28.55	100
Portuguese females	3,199	2,859	89.37	10.63	100
Japanese males	17,978	4,294	23.88	76.12	100
Japanese females	4,064	3,226	79.38	20.62	100
Chinese males	17,383	4,163	23.95	76.05	100
Chinese females	1,269	1,173	92.43	7.57	100
South Sea Island males	296	118	39.86	60.14	100
South Sea Island females	105	76	72.38	27.62	100
Other nationalities, males	355	162	45.63	54.37	100
Other nationalities, females	56	49	87.50	12.50	100
Total males	57,278	21,806	38.07	61.93	100
Total females	22,021	17,969	81.60	18.40	100
Total of all	79,299	39,775	50.16	49.84	100

Y

HAWAIIAN-AMERICA

MATERNITY STATISTICS

Nationalities	Number of Females	Number Over 15 Years of Age	Per cent. Over 15 Years of Age	Number of Married	Per cent. of Married to All Over 15 Years	Number of Mothers	Per cent. of Mothers to All Over 15	Number of Children Born	Average of Children to Each Mother	Number of Children Surviving	Per cent. of Children Surviving
Hawaiians	14,620	9,778	66.88	8,215	84.01	5,805	59.36	27,994	4.82	16,659	59.50
Part Hawaiians	4,236	1,727	40.76	1,120	64.85	904	52.34	4,031	4.45	3,028	75.12
Hawaiian-born foreigners	6,675	444	6.65	199	44.82	154	34.68	545	3.54	484	88.80
Americans	692	592	85.54	421	71.11	294	49.66	941	3.20	731	77.68
British	484	436	90.08	357	81.88	260	59.63	1,158	4.45	885	76.25
Germans	298	258	86.57	212	82.17	174	67.44	776	4.69	610	78.60
French	29	28	96.55	8	28.57	3	10.71	18	6.00	11	61.11
Norwegians	71	65	91.54	54	83.07	46	70.77	204	4.43	168	82.35
Portuguese	3,636	3,199	87.98	2,859	89.34	2,327	72.42	13,222	5.68	9,476	71.67
Japanese	4,171	4,064	97.43	3,226	79.38	1,510	37.15	2,499	1.65	2,218	88.75
Chinese	1,419	1,269	89.42	1,173	92.43	844	66.50	2,436	2.88	2,133	87.56
South Sea Islanders	109	105	96.33	76	72.38	34	32.38	76	2.23	49	64.47
Other nationalities	63	56	88.88	49	87.50	36	64.28	139	3.86	119	85.61
Total	36,503	22,021	60.32	17,969	81.60	12,391	56.26	54,039	4.36	36,569	67.67

CLASSIFICATION OF POPULATION BY NATIONALITIES AND RELIGIONS

Nationalities	Totals	Per cent. of Protestants	Per cent. of Catholics	Per Cent. of Mormons	Total Per cent.
Hawaiians	25,637	50.09	32.87	17.04	100
Part-Hawaiians	6,271	51.70	41.99	6.31	100
Haw.-born foreigners	8,438	21.34	78.48	.18	100
Americans	1,650	85.09	12.85	2.06	100
British	1,371	86.36	13.13	.51	100
Germans	677	87.44	12.26	.30	100
French	63	9.54	90.46	—	100
Norwegians	162	95.06	4.94	—	100
Portuguese	7,959	1.84	98.15	.01	100
Japanese	764	93.06	6.42	.52	100
Chinese	953	87.83	7.03	5.14	100
South Sea Islanders	223	79.82	18.83	1.35	100
Other nationalities	354	49.72	48.30	1.98	100
Total	54,522	42.68	48.36	8.96	100

Deducting the above number, 54,522, from the whole population of 109,020, we find 54,498 who did not return themselves as of any religion. The Chinese and Japanese number 46,023. Of these 1717 return themselves in the above divisions. This leaves 44,306 who must be Buddhists, etc., and deducting this number from the total or 54,498 who made no returns, we have 10,192 of all other nationalities who either decline to state their religious belief, or profess no religion.

HAWAIIAN-AMERICA

LEPROSY

TABLE SHOWING THE NUMBER OF LEPERS AT THE SETTLEMENT ON MOLOKAI, MORTALITY, AND NUMBER ON THE BOOKS AT THE END OF EACH YEAR

Year	Admissions	Deaths	Discharged or Unaccounted for	Number on the Books Dec. 31st.
1866	141	26	10	105
1867	70	25	7	143
1868	115	28	2	228
1869	126	59	11	284
1870	57	58	4	279
1871	183	51	9	402
1872	105	64	4	439
1873	487	156	21	749
1874	91	161	8	671
1875	212	163	14	706
1876	96	122	3	677
1877	163	129	1	710
1878	239	147	—	802
1879	125	209	1	717
1880	51	152	10	606
1881	232	132	—	706
1882	71	121	6	649
1883	301	150	15	785
1884	108	168	8	717
1885	103	142	26	655
1886	43	100	8	590
1887	220	108	4	698
1888	579	212	28	1035
1889	308	149	7	1187
1890	202	158	18	1213
1891	143	212	2	1142
1892	109	137	19	1095
1893	211	151	—	1155
1894	128	155	3	1124
1894	106	128	15	1087
1896	146	116	2	1115
1897	124	139	—	1100

REAL ESTATE

REAL ESTATE

CLASSIFICATION BY NATIONALITY AND SEX OF OWNERS OF REAL ESTATE AND OWNERS OF HOMES

NATIONALITIES	OWN REAL ESTATE			OWN HOUSE THEY LIVE IN		
	Male	Female	Total	Male	Female	Total
Hawaiians	2,570	1,425	3,995	2,432	668	3,100
Part Hawaiians	400	322	722	305	151	456
Haw'n-born for'gners	98	62	160	44	24	68
Americans	220	53	273	164	28	192
British	198	53	251	134	33	167
Germans	83	11	94	87	9	96
French	10	—	10	7	1	8
Norwegians	24	3	27	19	1	20
Portuguese	393	45	438	645	50	695
Japanese	93	4	97	335	10	345
Chinese	190	5	195	745	13	758
South Sea Islanders	2	2	4	2	—	2
Other nationalities	57	4	61	56	3	59
Totals	4,338	1,989	6,327	4,975	991	5,966

The total real-estate owners reporting themselves in 1890 was 4695; while the total real-estate owners reporting in 1896 was 6327, an increase of 1632 owners. This increase is due to the homesteaders, and the main part of it is divided among the Hawaiians, part Hawaiians, and Portuguese. These three nationalities report as follows:

NATIONALITIES	1890	1896	Increase
Hawaiian owners of real estate	3,271	3,995	724
Part Hawaiian owners of real estate	395	722	327
Portuguese owners of real estate	234	438	204
Ten other nations, owners of real estate	795	1,172	377

There are in all 5966 houses owned by the persons inhabiting them. So that out of the 13,724 residences on the islands, 43.46 per cent. are dwelt in by their owners. Of these dwellings the

HAWAIIAN-AMERICA

Hawaiians own...................... 51.94 per cent.
Part Hawaiians own.................. 7.64 per cent.
Portuguese own...................... 11.64 per cent.
Chinese own......................... 12.70 per cent.
Japanese own........................ 5.78 per cent.
Eight other nationalities own .... 10.30 per cent.

The percentage of the population occupying the different classes of houses is as follows:

3,488 Plantation quarters contain	29.58
25 Jails and lock-ups contain	.49
23 Hospitals and asylums contain	.40
114 Hotels and boarding-houses contain	.78
205 Lodging-houses contain.................	1.86
16 Boarding-schools contain................	.93
14,026 Private residences contain...............	65.87
1 Drill shed / 1 Barracks	.09
	100.00

PUBLIC LANDS

RECAPITULATION HAWAIIAN PUBLIC LANDS

	Rice	Coffee	Cane	Pasture	Forest and Mountain or Waste Land	Value
Hawaii	140	62,890	18,156	368,849	749,302	$1,874,900
Mau	110	8,180	520	112,570	58,550	453,800
Oahu	327	800	2,050	71,414	13,778	983,500
Kauai	400	4,400	4,900	80,050	86,650	648,000
Molokai	—	—	—	40,625	—	77,500
Lanai & Kahoolawe ..	—	—	—	77,669	—	70,000
	977	76,270	25,626	751,177	908,280	4,107,700

EDUCATIONAL

CLASSIFICATION BY NATIONALITY OF THOSE ABLE TO READ AND WRITE

Nationalities	Number Over 6 Years	Per cent. Literacy
Hawaiian	26,495	83.97
Part Hawaiian	5,895	91.21
Hawaiian-born foreigners	5,394	68.29
Americans	2,060	86.02
British	1,516	95.44
Germans	899	86.31
French	75	92.00
Norwegians	215	80.46
Portuguese	8,089	27.84
Japanese	22,189	53.60
Chinese	19,317	48.47
South Sea Islanders	407	40.05
Other nationalities	423	75.41

ATTENDING SCHOOL

Nationalities	Number Within School Age	Per cent. Attending School
Hawaiians	5,467	98.39
Part Hawaiians	2,437	99.01
Hawaiian-born foreigners	4,505	94.40
Americans	126	86.50
British	72	82.75
Germans	62	82.25
French	1	Over
Norwegians	12	100.00
Portuguese	774	85.40
Japanese	147	94.55
Chinese	665	92.48
South Sea Islanders	6	Over
Other nationalities	12	83.33
Total	14,286	96.20

HAWAIIAN-AMERICA

RETROSPECTIVE

1884—Number within school age, 12,333.
                        Percentage attending school, 70.73.
1890—Number within school age, 12,099.
                        Percentage attending school, 81.59.
1896—Number within school age, 14,286.
                        Percentage attending school, 96.20.

YEAR	Number Over 6 Years	Per cent. Literacy
1884	70,382	55.43
1890	78,571	48.85
1896	93,105	63.90

NUMBER OF SCHOOLS, CLASS, COMPILED 1898

ISLANDS	*GOVERNMENT SCHOOLS					INDEPENDENT SCHOOLS		
	No. of Schools	No. of Teachers	No. of Pupils, Boys	No. of Pupils, Girls	Total No. of Pupils	No. of Schools	No. of Teachers	No. of Pupils
Hawaii	48	90	1,700	1,462	3,162	12	32	666
Oahu	36	108	2,224	1,618	3,842	37	148	2,586
Maui and Lanai	28	59	1,100	850	1,950	8	20	538
Kauai and Niihau	15	35	811	646	1,457	3	9	164
Molokai	5	6	90	67	157	—	—	—
Totals	132	298	5,925	4,643	10,568	60	209	3,954

* Of government schools taught in Hawaiian there is now but one, with a total of 26 pupils.

COMPARATIVE TABLE OF SCHOOL POPULATION,
1897-98
(From Reports of the Department of Education)

Islands	No. Schools 1898	IN SCHOOL, JAN., 1898			No. Schools 1897	IN SCHOOL, JAN., 1897		
		Boys	Girls	Total		Boys	Girls	Total
Hawaii......	60	2,055	1,773	3,828	64	2,008	1,703	3,711
Maui & Lanai	36	1,321	1,167	2,488	37	1,319	1,151	2,470
Molokai.....	5	90	67	157	6	114	64	178
Oahu	73	3,638	2,790	6,427	71	3,429	2,670	6,099
Kauai & Niihau......	18	913	708	1,621	17	878	687	1,565
Totals....	192	8,017	6,505	14,522	195	7,748	6,275	14,023

NUMBER OF SCHOOLS, TEACHERS, AND PUPILS

	Schools	Teachers		Total	Pupils		Total
		M.	F.		M.	F.	
Public Schools, English.	131	122	175	297	5,908	4,634	10,542
Public Schools Taught in Hawaiian..........	1	1	—	1	17	9	26
Private Schools........	60	82	127	209	2,092	1,862	3,954
Total.............	192	205	302	507	8,017	6,505	14,522

HAWAIIAN-AMERICA

NATIONALITY OF PUPILS ATTENDING SCHOOL IN THE HAWAIIAN ISLANDS. COMPARATIVE TABLE FOR THE YEARS 1888, 1890, 1892, 1894, 1895, 1896, 1897

	1888	1890	1892	1894	1895	1896	1897
Hawaiian..	5,320	5,599	5,353	5,177	5,207	5,480	5,330
Part Hawaiian..	1,247	1,573	1,866	2,103	2,198	2,443	2,479
American..	253	259	371	285	386	417	484
British....	163	139	131	184	200	259	280
German...	176	199	197	208	253	288	302
Portuguese	1,335	1,813	2,253	2,551	186	3,600	3,815
Sc'dinavian	40	56	71	83	96	98	106
French....	—	1	5	5	8	2	2
Japanese..	54	39	60	113	261	397	560
Chinese...	147	262	353	529	740	931	1,078
South Sea Islanders	16	42	36	35	29	23	10
Other foreigners	19	24	16	34	52	88	76
Total ...	8,770	10,006	10,712	11,307	12,616	14,023	14,522

COMPARATIVE TABLE OF THE NATIONALITIES OF TEACHERS IN ALL SCHOOLS OF THE HAWAIIAN ISLANDS

	1892	1894	1895	1896	1897
Hawaiian................	93	80	68	68	57
Part Hawaiian............	47	61	60	59	62
American................	154	155	177	226	253
British..................	57	57	66	76	69
German.................	9	4	8	8	12
French..................	9	7	6	5	6
Belgian.................	4	5	5	7	—
Scandinavian............	5	7	5	6	6
Dutch...................	—	1	2	1	—
Portuguese..............	8	10	13	13	20
Japanese................	—	1	2	2	3
Chinese.................	4	17	14	11	13
Other foreigners.........	2	—	—	—	6
Total................	392	405	426	482	507

INDUSTRIAL

PERCENTAGE OF NATIONALITIES ENGAGED IN INDUSTRIAL PURSUITS

Nationalities	Total Male Population over 15 years	Laborers	Ranchers and Agriculturists	Fishers	Mariners	Mechanics	Drivers and Teamsters	Merchants and Traders	Clerks and Salesmen	Professions	Other Occupations	Total with Occupations
Hawaiians	11,250	24.51	33.02	7.75	2.84	4.56	1.48	.32	1.19	1.17	4.95	81.79
Part Hawaiians	1,731	20.12	13.58	2.19	1.33	14.17	2.43	1.45	8.44	3.12	12.02	78.85
Americans	1,621	3.64	6.85	.06	12.71	17.89	2.34	7.10	15.11	12.10	16.84	94.64
British	1,120	5.89	9.01		4.64	23.66	1.87	9.01	16.61	7.23	15.92	93.84
Germans	605	26.34	8.59		2.64	18.67	3.30	5.28	11.23	3.13	20.82	100.00
French	48	16.66	6.25		14.58	20.83		4.16	6.25	22.91	12.50	100.00
Norwegians	142	13.38	10.57		11.27	24.65	3.52	2.81	5.63		14.79	86.62
Portuguese	4,187	72.51	9.36	.24	.22	6.14	2.25	2.03	1.89	.71	3.20	98.55
Japanese	17,980	80.10	3.51	.50	.10	1.45	.26	1.31	.88	.48	2.89	91.48
Chinese	17,445	62.61	12.14	1.69	.09	1.26	.60	4.70	1.68	1.80	8.65	95.22
S. S. Islanders	297	57.58	7.08	2.36	5.72	1.01	.67	.34		.34	2.35	77.45
Other foreigners	372	22.85	11.29	3.50	15.06	14.25	1.34	4.30	4.57	4.03	16.40	97.59

HAWAIIAN-AMERICA

Taking up the matter of the labor of all the nationalities, it will be seen that the bulk of the unskilled labor is performed by the Japanese and Chinese, these races supplying 27,499 laborers, against 6939 of all other nationalities. That is to say, out of a total of 34,438 unskilled laborers, the percentages are as follows:

The Japanese have	16,588	or 48.1	per cent.
The Chinese have	10,941	or 31.8	per cent.
The Portuguese have	3,119	or 9.1	per cent.
The Hawaiians have	2,837	or 8.2	per cent.
All other nationalities have	953	or 2.8	per cent.
Total	34,438	or 100.00	per cent.

PLANTATION LABOR STATISTICS

NUMBER AND NATIONALITY OF THE SUGAR PLANTATION LABORERS

(Compiled from the latest Report of the Secretary of the Bureau of Immigration, December 31, 1897)

Islands	Hawaiians	Portuguese	Japanese	Chinese	S. S. Islanders	All Others	Total
Hawaii	425	952	5,021	2,995	20	267	9,680
Maui	534	496	2,031	1,529	36	156	4,782
Oahu	242	211	1,691	1,687	2	31	3,864
Kauai	296	559	3,325	1,903	23	221	6,327
Total 1897	1,497	2,218	12,068	8,114	81	675	24,653
" 1896	1,615	2,268	12,893	7,289	115	600	23,780
Decrease 1897	118	50	725	—	34	—	—
Increase 1897	—	—	—	6,825	—	75	873

RAILROADS

RAILROADS

There are three railroads on the Hawaiian Islands: One on Maui, running from Kahului via Wailuku for about fifteen miles along the coast to Paia; one on Hawaii, from Mahukona to Niulii, about twenty miles; and the Oahu line, on Oahu, which is now operating from Honolulu to Waialua, a distance of fifty-five miles, is soon to be extended to Waimea, a few miles farther, and by the last of the present year will be around the northern extremity of the island, so far as Kahuku. This road was opened June 1, 1890, and is largely responsible for the development of Oahu's present large sugar industry. It is well equipped, with excellent road-bed and rolling-stock; carried 60,000 passengers in 1898, and is prospering.

COMPARATIVE VIEW OF COMMERCE OF HAWAIIAN ISLANDS FROM 1867, GIVING TOTALS FOR EACH YEAR

Revised and Compared with Recent Official Tables

Year	Total Imports	Total Exports	Domestic Produce Exported	Foreign Produce Exported	Total Custom-house Receipts	National Ves. No.	Shipping Mer. Vessels No.	Shipping Mer. Vessels Tons	Whal. No.	Spirits Gallons Cons'd	Haw. Reg. Vessels No.	Haw. Reg. Vessels Tons
1867	$1,957,410	$1,679,662	$1,324,122	$355,540	$220,599	11	134	60,268	243	15,119	77	11,456
1868	1,935,791	1,898,215	1,450,269	447,946	210,076	7	113	54,833	153	16,030	63	9,793
1869	2,040,680	2,366,359	1,743,292	623,067	215,798	6	127	75,656	102	17,016	61	10,528
1870	1,930,227	2,144,942	1,514,425	630,517	223,815	16	159	91,248	118	19,948	64	10,955
1871	1,625,884	2,892,069	1,733,094	1,158,975	221,332	9	171	105,993	47	18,817	57	8,068
1872	1,746,178	1,607,522	1,402,685	204,837	218,375	7	146	98,647	47	18,843	54	6,407
1873	1,437,611	2,128,054	1,725,507	402,547	198,655	12	109	62,767	63	21,212	58	8,561
1874	1,310,827	1,839,620	1,622,455	217,165	183,857	13	120	71,266	43	18,466	54	8,101
1875	1,682,471	2,089,736	1,835,383	254,353	213,447	22	120	93,110	41	21,131	51	7,376
1876	1,811,770	2,241,041	2,055,133	185,908	199,236	14	141	108,706	37	19,707	45	6,753
1877	2,554,356	2,676,202	2,462,417	213,786	230,499	17	168	116,621	33	24,223	54	8,994
1878	3,046,370	3,548,472	3,333,979	214,492	284,426	11	232	163,640	27	36,360	55	7,949
1879	3,742,978	3,781,718	3,665,504	116,214	359,671	6	251	151,576	25	43,166	63	10,023
1880	3,673,268	4,068,445	3,989,194	79,251	402,182	15	239	141,916	16	44,289	63	10,149
1881	4,547,979	6,855,436	6,789,076	66,360	423,192	13	258	159,341	19	46,085	60	9,338
1882	4,974,510	8,299,017	8,165,931	133,085	505,391	6	258	172,619	32	50,064	60	9,351
1883	5,624,240	8,133,344	8,036,227	97,117	577,333	13	267	185,316	18	61,272	64	11,589
1884	4,637,514	8,856,610	8,067,649	788,961	551,737	11	241	187,826	23	79,160	53	9,826
1885	3,830,545	9,158,818	8,958,664	200,154	502,337	6	253	190,138	26	80,115	51	9,250
1886	4,877,738	10,565,886	10,340,375	225,510	580,444	6	310	222,372	20	100,703	58	13,529
1887	4,943,841	9,707,047	9,435,204	271,843	595,003	13	254	210,703	23	74,913	57	12,244
1888	4,540,887	11,707,599	11,631,435	76,164	546,143	18	240	221,143	17	68,247	61	15,406
1889	5,438,791	13,874,341	13,810,070	64,271	559,010	20	271	218,785	19	74,816	57	15,403
1890	6,962,201	13,142,829	13,023,304	119,525	695,957	13	295	230,120	21	88,884	55	14,222
1891	7,439,583	10,258,788	10,107,316	151,473	732,595	11	310	284,155	17	88,536	51	13,430
1892	4,028,295	8,060,087	7,959,938	100,149	494,385	10	262	238,622	20	86,441	50	13,851
1893	4,363,178	10,818,158	10,742,658	75,500	545,754	13	315	323,685	17	46,428	53	19,505
1894	5,104,481	9,140,795	9,053,310	87,485	522,855	15	350	343,844	19	41,136	53	21,495
1895	5,339,785	8,474,138	8,358,107	116,031	547,149	8	318	337,817	10	39,653	52	21,679
1896	6,036,652	15,515,230	15,436,037	79,193	656,896	14	386	477,997	5	44,168	59	29,024
1897	7,682,628	16,021,775	15,933,689	88,086	708,493	—	427	513,820	—	53,345	62	34,069

COMMERCIAL

COMPARATIVE TABLE OF PRINCIPAL ARTICLES OF EXPORT, 1867 TO 1897

Year	Sugar, Lbs.	Molasses, Gallons	Rice, Lbs.	Paddy, Lbs.	Coffee, Lbs.	Hides, Pieces	Tallow, Lbs.	Goat Skins	Wool, Lbs.	Pulu, Lbs.	Fungus, Lbs.	Salt, Tons	Guano, Tons	Pine-apples, Pcs.	Bananas Bunches	Total Value all Domestic Exp'ts
1867	17,127,187	544,994	441,750	572,099	127,546	11,207	60,936	51,889	409,471	203,958	167,666	107			2,913	$1,324,122.02
1868	18,312,926	492,839	40,450	862,954	78,373	11,144	109,504	57,670	268,914	342,882	76,781	540			3,966	1,450,269.26
1869	18,302,110	338,311	48,830	1,586,959	340,841	12,803	85,937	62,736	218,752	622,998	85,215	1,152			6,936	1,713,091.59
1870	18,783,639	216,662	152,068	535,453	415,111	13,095	90,388	67,463	234,696	213,803	41,968	2,513			4,007	1,514,425.06
1871	21,760,773	271,291	417,011	867,452	46,990	19,384	185,240	58,900	471,706	202,720	37,475	711			3,876	1,733,094.46
1872	16,995,402	192,105	455,121	894,582	39,276	27,066	493,978	53,598	288,526	284,127	32,161	522			4,520	1,402,685.38
1873	23,129,101	146,459	941,438	262,025	20,677	609,855	66,702	329,507	421,283	57,538	445			6,492	1,721,507.78	
1874	24,566,611	90,060	1,187,986	507,945	125,596	71,955	399,926	418,320	50,955	730½			6,394	1,622,455.37		
1875	25,080,182	93,722	1,573,739	439,157	75,406	20,620	721,590	60,598	565,469	379,903	45,098	96			10,518	1,835,382.91
1876	26,072,429	39,073	2,259,324	556,495	165,977	22,777	851,920	45,265	405,542	314,432	14,982	5			15,995	2,055,133.55
1877	25,575,965	151,469	2,691,370	1,542,603	153,667	22,164	327,291	51,551	385,703	150,586	11,629	322			13,431	2,402,462.66
1878	38,431,458	93,136	2,767,768	1,101,345	22,164	309,826	239,941	64,525	522,757	212,740	22,364	180¼			3,333,979.49		
1879	49,020,972	87,475	4,792,813	2,784,861	127,963	25,309	24,885	24,940	464,308	137,001	2,557	50			12,369	3,605,503.76
1880	63,584,871	198,355	6,469,840	38,815	74,275		31,013	381,316	44,846	14,801	14½			19,164	4,889,194.40	
1881	93,789,483	263,587	7,682,700	99,508	22,945	118,031	21,308	528,489	53,415	2,570	302			20,776	6,780,076.38	
1882	114,177,938	221,293	12,159,475	102,370	18,912	21,972	77,898	23,402	528,913		4,282			28,848	8,165,931.34	
1883	114,107,155	193,997	11,619,000	459,633	8,131	26,007	34,252	244,798	318,271		2,111			44,902	8,036,227.11	
1884	142,654,923	110,530	1,368,705	16,057	38,955	20,125	407,623		3,783			58,040	8,067,648.82			
1885	171,350,314	57,941	9,493,000	46,224	4,231	21,026	2,864			2,247			60,046	8,958,663.88		
1886	216,223,615	13,137	7,367,253	1,675	19,045		19,782	474,121	465	1,137			45,862	9,346,375.17		
1887	212,763,647	71,222	7,338,615	5,931	31,207	21,395	21,173	418,784					58,936	9,435,204.12		
1888	235,888,346	47,965	12,878,600	5,300	28,639	56,713	16,233	75,911					71,335	11,631,434.88		
1889	242,165,835	54,612	9,669,896	43,673	27,158	204,743	17,589	56,289					105,030	13,810,070.54		
1890	259,798,462	74,926	10,579,000	400	88,593	28,196	97,125	125	241,925					97,204	13,023,304.16	
1891	274,983,580	55,845	4,900,450	3,051	28,196	33,876	8,661	374,724			5,368			116,766	10,107,315.67	
1892	263,656,715	47,988	11,516,328	13,568	26,427	27,225	7,316	97,119			40,171	61		105,375	10,742,658.05	
1893	330,684,879	67,282	7,821,004	49,311	19,826	792	3,449	288,969			19,042	1,217		108,239	7,959,938.05	
1894	330,822,879	72,979	7,803,972	180,150	19,826	13,250	5,911	391,592			44,903			123,006	9,053,309.87	
1895	294,784,993	44,970	3,768,762	118,755	21,603		6,759	261,337			44,903			105,055	8,358,106.79	
1896	443,569,282	15,881	5,025,491	255,655	19,180		6,466	227,987			65,213			126,413	15,436,037.23	
1897	520,158,232	33,770	5,499,499	337,158	25,079	9,000	12,647	462,819			147,451			75,835	16,021,775.19	

HAWAIIAN-AMERICA

TABLE OF QUANTITY AND VALUE OF HAWAIIAN EXPORTS TO ALL COUNTRIES FOR THE YEAR 1897.

Articles	United States * 99.62 per cent.		Australia and New Zealand .12 per cent.		Is. of Pacific, China and Japan .11 per cent.		Canada .15 per cent.		Total 100.00 per cent.	
	Quantity	Value	Qua'ty	Value	Qua'ty	Value	Qua'ty	Value	Quantity	Value
Sugar...........lbs.	520,532,192	$15,390,223.09	3,200	$ 126.00	1,623	$ 73.04	—	—	520,158,232	$15,390,422.13
Rice............lbs.	5,448,700	225,055.60	—	—	10,799	519.92	—	—	5,499,499	225,575.52
Coffee..........lbs.	288,228	89,813.36	27,273	5,803.00	395	58.90	21,352	4,021.36	337,158	99,696.62
Bananas...bunches	74,759	74,364.50	—	—	18	12.00	1,068	1,036.00	75,835	75,412.50
Wool............lbs.	204,720	17,759.44	—	—	—	—	44,480	3,558.40	249,200	21,308.84
Hides............pcs.	25,140	87,545.48	—	—	—	—	—	—	25,140	87,545.48
Pineapples......pcs.	125,012	11,946.25	3,083	263.05	—	—	21,420	2,213.87	149,515	14,423.17
Goat-skins.....pcs.	6,085	2,055.00	—	—	—	—	—	—	6,085	2,055.00
Sheep-skins....pcs.	9,907	2,711.95	—	—	—	—	—	—	9,907	2,711.95
Tallow..........lbs.	9,000	225.00	—	—	—	—	750	93.00	33,770	225.00
Molasses.......gals.	33,020	2,799.72	—	—	—	—	—	—	9,000	2,892.72
Betel Leaves..boxes	145	509.00	—	—	—	—	—	—	145	509.00
Taro Flour......sks.	218	267.50	—	—	—	—	—	—	218	267.50
Plants, Seeds..pcs.	40,752	1,735.40	2	5.25	—	—	—	—	40,754	1,740.65
Sundry Fruit.value	—	369.00	—	—	3.00	—	—	—	—	572.00
Awa............pkgs.	6	27.49	—	—	—	—	—	—	6	27.49
Hones and Horns..	105,235	665.80	—	—	—	—	—	—	105,235	665.80
Curios.........pkgs.	11	168.50	14	351.00	1	3.00	—	66.00	26	588.50
Canned Fruits...cs.	72	165.40	—	—	—	—	45	182.50	115	347.90
Sundries......pkgs.	—	648.66	24	985.70	14	33.85	—	40.00	51	1,708.21
Honey..........lbs.	13	648.00	—	7,635.71	—	18,571.56	—	—	476	
" "...........lbs.	108	51,143.04	—	—	—	—	3,960	198.00	53,020	4,993.00
Foreign Products...	—	—	368 49,060	4,147.00	—	—	—	9,744.90	—	88,086.21
Total.........	—	$10,689,030.80	—	$19,316.71	—	$19,275.27	—	$21,154.03	—	$16,021,775.19

* Of this division U. S. Atlantic ports took 177,373,960 lbs. Sugar, valued at $6,272,007.38, or 32.90 per cent. of total value of exports for the year.

COMMERCIAL

SELECTIONS FROM CUSTOM-HOUSE TABLES, 1897

Value of Imports

Articles	Value Goods Paying Duty	Value Goods Free By Treaty	Value Goods Free By Civil Code	Total
Ale, Porter, Beer, Cider...	$ 81,076.75	—	$ 10.00	$ 81,068.75
Animals and Birds........	940.28	$ 100,583.50	4,042.54	105,565.87
Building Materials........	93,948.25	74,656.10	1,253.69	169,858.04
Clothing, Hats, Boots.....	141,786.55	225,167.74	3,477.25	370,431.54
Coal and Coke............	—	4,953.91	131,515.56	136,469.47
Crockery, Glassware, Lamps, etc...............	48,973.19	—	255.41	49,229.25
Drugs, Surgical Instruments, and Dental Materials...................	74,587.74	—	153.50	74,741.50
Dry Goods { Cottons......	100,283.08	241,126.77	11.13	341,420.98
Linens......	21,235.27	—	—	21,235.27
Silks........	24,349.70	—	—	24,349.70
Woollens	71,923.36	8,596.91	965.24	81,485.51
Mixtures	26,662.62	849.79	—	27,512.41
Fancy Goods, Millinery, etc......................	110,188.87	16,768.39	369.00	127,326.26
Fertilizer, Bone-meal, etc..	—	—	402,756.25	402,756.25
Fish (dried and salt)......	33,415.11	76,412.57	—	109,827.68
Flour.....................	4,993.86	226,277.99	—	231,271.85
Fruits (fresh)	1,551.21	15,144.92	5.00	16,701.13
Furniture.................	40,981.97	63,417.51	1,296.00	105,695.48
Grain and Feed...........	26.93	368,808.82	116.69	368,952.44
Groceries and Provisions..	236,056.31	371,567.64	1,876.26	609,500.21
Guns and Gun Materials..	11,813.61	3,674.57	662.42	16,150.60
Gunpowder...............	15,814.66	—	630.39	16,445.05
Hardware, Agricultural Implements, and Tools.....	70,400.53	320,214.12	14,921.80	405,536.45
Iron, Steel, etc...........	12,216.46	45,972.86	8,473.42	66,662.74
Jewelry, Plate, Clocks	30,549.83	—	580.00	31,129.83
Leather	1,761.03	41,248.34	—	43,009.37
Lumber	3,715.55	285,027.65	125.76	288,868.96
Machinery................	102,265.49	484,927.38	8,230.95	595,423.82
Matches..................	1,083.45	12,665.37	—	13,748.82
Musical Instruments......	5,206.66	10,833.02	925.00	16,964.68
Naval Stores..............	8,071.40	50,434.38	20,650.01	79,156.79
Oils (cocoanut, kerosene, whale, etc.)...............	24,104.91	70,623.49	941.84	95,670.24
Paints, Paint Oil, and Turpentine..................	64,845.78	2,160.05	612.97	67,618.80
Perfumery and Toilet Articles.....................	13,523.66	7,759.02	—	21,282.68
Railroad Materials, Rails, Cars, etc..................	59,438.62	56,879.92	—	116,318.54
Saddlery, Carriages, and Materials.................	70,712.66	53,663.18	3,314.10	127,689.94
Sheathing Metal..........	—	1,254.38	696.44	1,950.82
Shooks, Bags, and Containers.....................	205,749.93	14,037.56	14,229.34	234,016.83
Spirits	2,083.93	—	188.08	2,272.01
Stationery and Books.....	14,145.20	77,206.80	7,158.31	98,510.31
Tea......................	33,882.32	—	—	33,882.32

Z 353

HAWAIIAN-AMERICA

Selections from Custom-House Tables, 1897.—*Continued*.

Articles	Value Goods Paying Duty	Value Goods Free By Treaty	Value Goods Free By Civil Code	Total
Tin, Tinware, and Materials	$ 11,158.97	—	$ 411.10	$ 11,570.07
Tobacco, Cigars, etc.	32,276.40	$139,467.79	989.90	172,734.09
Wines (light)	57,476.87	—	79,763.38	137,240.25
Sundry Personal and Household Effects	4,444.70	—	42,220.57	46,665.27
Sundry Merchandise not included in the above	129,405.16	71,089.47	21,877.42	222,372.05
Charges on invoices	66,633.87	32,057.96	2,060.48	102,053.31
25 per cent. added on Uncertified Invoices	1,087.32	—	—	1,087.32
	$2,166,850.02	$3,575,529.47	$ 777,768.20	$6,520,147.64
Discounts	15,916.03	2,488.52	166.12	18,570.67
Total at Honolulu	$2,150,933.93	$3,573,040.90	$ 777,602.08	$6,538,718.31
Total at Hilo	43,196.12	384,728.47	122,299.49	550,224.08
Total at Kahului	30,077.74	226,700.50	58,608.20	316,386.44
Total at Mahukona	10,028.54	133,474.43	31,662.66	175,165.63
Value Goods in Bond, net	—	—	—	139,274.97
Total Hawaiian Islands	$2,234,236.39	$4,318,944.30	$ 990,172,43	$7,682,628.09
Specie	—	—	1,155,575.00	—

HAWAIIAN SUGAR PLANTATION STATISTICS
From 1875 to 1897, inclusive

Year	SUGAR		MOLASSES		Total Export Value
	Pounds	Value	Gallons	Value	
1875	25,080,182	$1,216,388.82	93,722	$12,183.86	$ 1,228,572.68
1876	26,072,429	1,272,334.53	130,073	19,510.95	1,291,845.48
1877	25,575,965	1,777,529.57	151,462	22,719.30	1,800,248.87
1878	38,431,458	2,701,731.60	93,136	12,107.68	2,713,839.18
1879	49,020,972	3,109,563.66	87,475	9,622.52	3,119,185.91
1880	63,584,871	4,322,711.48	198,355	29,753.52	4,352,464.73
1881	93,789,483	5,395,399.54	263,587	31,630.44	5,427,020.98
1882	114,177,938	6,320,890.65	221,293	33,193.95	6,354,084.60
1883	114,107,155	7,112,981.12	193,997	34,819.46	7,147,800.58
1884	142,654,923	7,328,896.67	110,530	16,579.50	7,345,476.17
1885	171,350,314	8,356,061.94	57,941	7,050.00	8,363,111.94
1886	216,223,615	9,775,132.12	113,137	14,501.76	9,789,633.88
1887	212,763,647	8,694,964.07	71,222	10,522.76	8,705,486.83
1888	235,888,346	10,818,883.09	47,965	5,900.40	10,824,783.49
1889	242,165,835	13,089,302.10	54,612	6,185.10	13,095,487.20
1890	259,789,462	12,159,585.01	74,926	7,603.29	12,167,188.30
1891	274,983,580	9,550,537.80	55,845	4,721.40	6,555,258.20
1892	263,636,715	7,276,549.24	47,988	5,061.07	7,281,610.34
1893	330,822,879	10,200,958.37	67,282	5,928.96	10,206,887.33
1894	306,684,993	8,473,009.10	72,979	6,050.11	8,479,059.21
1895	294,784,819	7,975,590.41	44,970	3,037.83	7,978,628.24
1896	443,569,282	14,932,172.82	15,885	1,209.72	14,933,382.54
1897	520,158,232	15,390,122.13	33,770	2,892.72	15,393,314.85

COMMERCIAL

HAWAII'S ANNUAL TRADE BALANCE, ETC., SINCE 1879

Revised and compared with recent official tables

Year	Imports	Exports	Excess Export Values	Custom-House Receipts
1880	$3,673,268.41	$4,968,444.87	$1,295,176.46	$402,181.63
1881	4,547,978.64	6,885,436.56	2,337,457.92	423,192.01
1882	4,974,510.01	8,299,016.70	3,324,506.69	505,390.98
1883	5,624,240.09	8,133,343.88	2,509,103.79	577,332.87
1884	4,637,514.22	8,856,610.30	4,219,096.08	551,736.59
1885	3,830,544.58	9,158,818.01	5,328,273.43	502,337.38
1886	4,877,738.73	10,565,885.58	5,688,146.85	580,444.04
1887	4,943,840.72	9,707,047.33	4,763,206.61	595,002.64
1888	4,540,887.46	11,707,598.76	7,166,711.30	546,142.63
1889	5,438,790.63	13,874,341.40	8,435,560.77	550,010.16
1890	6,962,201.13	13,142,829.48	6,180,628.35	695,956.91
1891	7,439,482.65	10,258,788.27	2,819,305.62	732,594.93
1892	4,028,295.31	8,060,087.21	4,031,791.90	494,385.10
1893	4,363,177.58	10,818,158.09	6,454,980.51	545,754.16
1894	5,104,481.43	9,140,794.56	4,036,313.13	522,855.41
1895	5,339,785.04	8,474,138.15	3,134,353.11	547,149.04
1896	6,063,652.41	15,515,230.13	9,451,577.72	656,895.82
1897	7,682,628.09	16,021,775.19	8,339,147.10	708,493.05

BONDED DEBT, ETC., JANUARY 1, 1898

Under Loan Act of 1882........		6%	...$	34,200.00
" " " 1886........		6%	....	2,000,000.00
" " " 1888........		6%	....	190,000.00
" " " 1890........ 5% and 6%			....	124,100.00
" " " 1892........ 5% " 6%			....	119,400.00
" " " 1893........		6%	....	650,000.00
" " " 1896........		5%	....	562,000.00
				3,079,700.00
Due Postal Savings Bank Depositors..............				809,181.62
Total.......				$4,488,881.62

HAWAIIAN-AMERICA

TABLE OF RECEIPTS, EXPENDITURES, AND PUBLIC DEBT OF HAWAII, FOR BIENNIAL PERIODS

Compiled from various Finance Reports to the Legislature

Periods Ending March Up to 1894, Then Dec. 31	Revenue	Expenditures	Cash Balance in Treasury	Public Debt
1856	$ 419,228.16	$ 424,778.25	$ 28,096.84	$ 22,000.00
1858	537,223.86	599,879.61	349.24	60,679.13
1860	571,041.71	612,410.55	13,127.52	128,777.83
1862	528,039.92	606,893.33	507.40	188,671.86
1864	538,445.34	511,511.10	22,583.29	166,649.09
1866	721,104.30	566,241.02	169,059.34	182,974.60
1868	825,498.98	786,617.55	163,567.84	120,815.23
1870	834,112.65	930,550.29	61,580.20	126,568.68
1872	912,130.74	969,784.14	56,752.41	177,971.29
1874	1,136,523.95	1,192,511.79	764.57	355,050.76
1876	1,008,956.42	919,356.93	89,599.49	459,187.59
1878	1,151,713.45	1,110,471.90	130,841.04	444,800.00
1880	1,703,736.88	1,495,697.48	338,880.44	388,900.00
1882	2,070,259.94	2,282,599.33	126,541.05	299,020.00
1884	3,092,085.42	3,216,406.05	2,220.42	898,800.00
1886	3,010,654.61	3,003,700.18	9,174.85	1,065,600.00
1888	4,812,575.95	4,712,285.20	109,465.60	1,936,500.00
1890	3,632,196.85	3,250,510.35	491,152.10	2,599,502.94
1892	3,916,880.72	4,095,891.44	312,141.38	3,217,161.13
1894	3,587,204.98	3,715,232.83	184,113.53	3,471,459.87
1895	3,506,183.96	3,172,070.73	69,225.65	3,811,064.49
1897	5,042,504.94	4,654,926.27	456,804.43	3,679,700.00

POLITICAL

ELECTION REGISTRY

Last Election under Monarchy, February, 1892

Total registered voters 14,217
Total of those that voted 10,293

Of these: Hawaiians numbered 9931; Portuguese, 2232; Americans, 670; British, 572; Germans, 399.

CONSTITUTIONAL CONVENTION, MAY, 1894

First Convention held under Provisional Government

Total registered voters 4430

Of these: Natives and half-castes numbered 798; Americans, 616; Hawaiians foreign born, 264; British, 358; Germans, 242; Portuguese, 1639.

GENERAL ELECTION, SEPTEMBER 29, 1897

Eleven Months after Republican Flag was raised

Total registered voters 2693

Of these: Hawaiians numbered 1126; Americans, 409; British, 247; Germans, 180; Portuguese, 612; Norwegians, 36.

ADDENDA

IMPORTANT EVENTS IN DEVELOPMENT OF HAWAII

First cattle—Vancouver..1792-94   First Christian marriage...1822
First spelling-book........1822   First baptism.............1823

1837-39, great religious revival—15,000 native converts on first Sunday in July, 1838; 1705 baptized at Hilo, and in six years following 27,000 were admitted to churches. By 1863, 52,413 had been admitted to membership in Protestant churches.

Missionaries cured drunkenness, but it is now on the increase.

THE END

By STEPHEN BONSAL, Jr.

THE REAL CONDITION OF CUBA TO-DAY. Illustrated. Map. Post 8vo, Paper, 60 cents.

His book is a graphic description of present misery in Cuba and an earnest appeal for proper recognition of existing conditions. Mr. Bonsal adds not inconsiderably to our knowledge of Cuba and its inhabitants.—*Outlook*, N. Y.

MOROCCO AS IT IS, with an Account of Sir Charles Euan Smith's Recent Mission to Fez. Illustrated. Post 8vo, Cloth, $2 00.

The opportunity to see something of the country was unusually good, and Mr. Bonsal describes it in a lively and vivacious style.—*Atlantic Monthly.*

The book is not only full of information, attractively presented, but abounds in romance, humor, and pathos.—*Boston Transcript.*

This book is as readable as it is honest and right-minded, and is enriched by its illustrations.—*N. Y. Mail and Express.*

The narrative is full of interest, showing the reader, as it does, the real life of the people who once were so important a factor in the world's economy.—*Daily Advertiser*, Boston.

HARPER & BROTHERS, Publishers
NEW YORK AND LONDON

☞ *Either of the above works will be sent by mail, postage prepaid, to any part of the United States, Canada, or Mexico, on receipt of the price.*

By WILLIAM DINWIDDIE

PUERTO RICO: Its Conditions and Possibilities. With 64 Illustrations. Crown 8vo, $2 50.

Mr. Dinwiddie has made a thorough study of the people, the climate, and the natural resources, and this book will be indispensable to every one who is considering Puerto Rico as a field for industrial enterprise. The business opportunities for Americans in sugar-cane, tobacco, coffee, and small fruits are set forth at great length.

Mr. Dinwiddie gives the most complete and satisfactory information as to the expense and the best methods of conducting coffee, sugar, and small-fruit plantations, as well as the opportunities offered to American investors in railroads, tramways, ice-plants, cattle-raising, dairy-farming, and manufacturing. The cost of living and the price of labor are all set forth in detail. In addition to its practical value as the best hand-book of Puerto Rican agriculture and manufacturing, the volume contains a full description of the natural resources, physical features, vegetable and mineral wealth, climate, prevalent diseases, and hygienic precautions for preventing them. It is the best book of its kind.

HARPER & BROTHERS, Publishers

NEW YORK AND LONDON

☞ *The above work will be sent by mail, postage prepaid, to any part of the United States, Canada, or Mexico, on receipt of the price.*

www.ingramcontent.com/pod-product-compliance
Lightning Source LLC
Chambersburg PA
CBHW030401230426
43664CB00007BB/699